STUDIES IN PHILOSOPHY

XXV

FALSIFICATION AND BELIEF

by

ALASTAIR McKINNON
McGill University

1970
MOUTON
THE HAGUE · PARIS

© Copyright 1970 in The Netherlands.
Mouton & Co. N.V., Publishers, The Hague.

No part of this book may be translated or reproduced in any form, by print, photoprint, microfilm, or any other means, without written permission from the publishers.

LIBRARY OF CONGRESS CATALOG CARD NUMBER: 71-108141

Printed in The Netherlands by Mouton & Co., Printers, The Hague.

PREFACE

Most properly intellectual difficulties with religious belief in our time appear to rest ultimately upon two charges which have been made explicit in recent philosophical criticism and which, though distinct, are not entirely unrelated. The first of these is that religious claims are, as I have here expressed it, unfalsifiable and vacuous; the second is that the foundations of belief are, again in my own words, undemonstrated and indemonstrable. I believe that these charges are interesting and important but I am also convinced that they reflect both a failure to do justice to the nature and complexity of religious belief and an easy acceptance of certain familiar but doubtful theories about how language actually functions. By way of answer I have therefore attempted to describe some of the ways in which language is used in certain typically religious contexts. My purpose in doing so is to cast some doubt upon these theories and, more immediately, to show how these charges might be answered.

The outline of the argument of Chapter III appeared originally in the *American Philosophical Quarterly,* July, 1965 and, in yet briefer form, in the *Canadian Journal of Theology,* April, 1966. Similarly, that of Chapter IV appeared in *The Christian Scholar,* Spring, 1966. This work presents these arguments in much greater detail and in a form which I trust meets most of the objections urged at the time of their original appearance. Equally important, it presents for the first time a detailed discussion of the scientific model upon which our case, at least as here presented, actually rests. I am grateful to the respective editors of these journals for permission to use this material in the present work. I am also grateful to the Princeton University Press for permission to quote briefly from the English translation of Kierkegaard's *Concluding Unscientific Postscript* and to Basil Blackwell for permission to quote from Wittgenstein's *Philosophical Investigations*.

I wish to thank my colleagues and students for having listened to these arguments and, in certain cases, for having replied to them at length. In particular, I wish to thank my good friend and former colleague Professor Donald D. Evans for his interest and many helpful comments.

Mrs. L. G. Barnard kindly read the first three chapters from the point of view of literary style and I am thankful for her help in this connection. In this, as in all matters of content, I am of course solely responsible for the blemishes which remain.

I take this opportunity to record my thanks to the members of my family for the thoughtfulness they have shown me throughout the writing of this work; without their help and cooperation it would have been quite impossible. It is a joy to be able to dedicate it to them.

I record my thanks to McGill University for a small grant toward the cost of the final typing of this work.

McGill University
Montreal

Alastair McKinnon

CONTENTS

Preface 5

I   Two Charges 9

II   A Model from Science 23

III   Unfalsifiable and Vacuous 47

IV   Undemonstrated and Indemonstrable 70

V   Concluding Remarks 92

1

TWO CHARGES

Logical positivism has not disappeared entirely from the philosophical scene but clearly it no longer occupies the centre of the stage. Most contemporary philosophers have come to see that it is uninteresting and individious. Even the critics of religion are no longer content to dismiss belief and its utterances as simply meaningless and nonsensical. At least they no longer employ these particular terms. Instead, they urge two other charges which are considerably more subtle and sophisticated and which together may finally prove much more damaging. The present brief study is specifically concerned with these. It is intended as an answer to these charges or, failing that, as a contribution in this direction.

The first of these charges turns about the notion of falsification, the current counterpart of the familiar conception of empirical verification. Quite simply, it is that religious utterances are unfalsifiable and therefore vacuous. The reasoning behind this charge is obvious and simple. Though apparently intended as factual claims, such utterances are quite unlike ordinary empirical assertions. The latter, of course, are defeated or falsified by a single counter-instance. "All swans are white" is routed by the appearance of a single swan of any other colour and one who asserts this statement must surrender it in the face of conflicting evidence. But, the charge runs, religious utterances appear to be treated quite differently. Though they look like factual claims and are frequently advanced as such, nothing is ever allowed to tell finally against them. Here at least nothing is permitted to stand as a counter-instance. They are unfalsifiable and, because ostensibly factual, dishonest. They masquerade as genuine assertions or claims but refuse the crucial test of falsification appropriate thereto. They are therefore empty or vacuous, mere pseudo-assertions which in fact assert nothing at all.

This charge can also be expressed in terms of the notion of belief. In its most familiar sense, belief is the acceptance of a factual or at least quasi-factual proposition: it is the claim that there are no counter-instances. Thus conceived, belief is a relatively intelligible and straightforward notion. But religious belief refuses to be bound by this simple rule. Believers continue to assert their claims even in the face of apparently conclusive evidence against them. They are in fact like Job: they cling to their beliefs even when all that seems to have prompted them has been destroyed. Now we know what it means to believe an ordinary generalization but what could it mean to believe something in the presence of apparently clear counter-instances? In fact, can it mean anything at all?

The point of this charge is clearly illustrated in the following example. A young man who has been consistently well-favoured throughout his life asserts the claim "God is love". He means that he is a tender father, that he attends to our needs, perhaps even that he indulges our whims and fancies. Shortly, however, the young man learns that he is dying of cancer, that the remainder of his life will be spent in pain and suffering and that soon his wife and children will be left to fend for themselves. It is clear that he cannot now intend his utterance in any of its former senses. And it is further clear that he cannot supply a new instance of what is ordinarily called the meaning of "love". This looks like a perfect confirmation of the critics' charge. Since the young man's claim is no longer true in its original sense, and since he cannot provide an alternative one, it must in the final analysis be empty and vacuous. Form and appearance notwithstanding, it is not an assertion. It is not even a significant sound. It is much more like mere noise; perhaps, indeed, it is only whistling in the dark.

The second charge is much less frequently expressed and less explicitly stated. Indeed, it is rarely put forth in any clear or articulate form. It is, however, the underlying presupposition of much historical and contemporary criticism of religious belief. And, though connected with the preceding charge, it is in some ways more radical and damaging. It is not content simply to call attention to certain defects in the utterances of the believer. It holds that religious belief itself rests upon certain factual assumptions which not only have not yet been demonstrated but, the stronger claim, are in fact essentially indemonstrable. It holds that belief rests upon assumptions which cannot possibly be known as true and that the believer would, if he were quite honest, give up his belief. In short, it holds that the necessary foundations of religious belief are and must be lacking.

Though religious belief allegedly rests upon a number of such assumptions this charge looms most frequently in the discussions of the existence of God. Indeed, it is the underlying presupposition of most such discussions. Again, the critics' reasoning is obvious and plausible. The existence of God is the most fundamental assumption of religious belief. Before one can assent to any of its further claims he must first know or at least believe that God does in fact exist. Until this has been established the rest simply hangs suspended in the air. This is why the critics of religion have concentrated so much of their energy upon the traditional proofs. They assume that if these could be called into question religious belief would thereby have been effectively discredited.

The nature and significance of this charge is well illustrated by its most important and familiar counterpart in the history of philosophy. Hume and his followers appear to have believed that the inductive sciences rest upon certain factual claims concerning the nature of the external world and that science would not be justified or accredited unless and until these were demonstrated. They seem to have thought that our confidence in the generalizations of science would not be justified until we had established the truth of certain propositions such as "Every event has a cause" and "The future will resemble the past". In short, they held that science would not be philosophically respectable until its external or preliminary foundations had been secured. The critics of religion assume that the situation is precisely the same with respect to religious belief: they hold that it is unjustified and indefensible until its underlying and allegedly dubitable assumptions have been demonstrated. And, like the Humean critics of science, they are confident that their challenge can never be answered.

These two charges can be summarized briefly. The first holds that the utterances of believers are unfalsifiable and therefore vacuous. The second holds that belief rests upon certain fundamental assumptions which are undemonstrated and indemonstrable. These charges are independent but, perhaps more important, closely connected. The nature and extent of this connection will emerge in the course of our investigation.

Though these are admittedly serious and potentially damaging charges, it is doubtful if they are as clear and flawless as their sponsors imagine. The first is invidious in the same way as its more clearly positivist predecessor: it equates meaningfulness with falsifiability and so begs the question it presumes to settle. The second has its own distinctive confusions. It treats religious belief as assent to a body of propositions rather than as an ongoing interpretative activity. It requires demonstrations which, from its standpoint, cannot be provided. It presumes that the logical foundation of belief must itself be simply another item of belief. It presumes that religion is and must be based upon certain merely contingent truths. Despite all this it is nevertheless clear that these charges are or at least could be substantial and important. The first raises the possibility that the utterances to which the believer commits himself are nothing more than pious and indeed empty hopes. And the second suggests that his belief may be without any basis or justification whatsoever. These are serious charges which any conscientious believer must be concerned to have answered.

There can be little doubt that these charges are more fundamental and searching than their more familiar predecessors. The difference can be put, though perhaps too simply, in the following way. The charges of the past concerned the truth of the believer's claims or, in certain cases, the adequacy of their foundation. Believers were therefore mainly concerned to defend their claims and the critics generally satisfied to attack them. But the present charges raise the more fundamental question of the content, substance and nature of these claims. They do not ask the believer to show that what he believes is true so much as they require him to show precisely what it is which he believes. They do not challenge the truth of his claims so much as they require him to describe their logic and function. They do not ask him to tell how he knows so much as they require him to say precisely what it is, if anything, that he knows.

This change can be illustrated with reference to the historic discussions of the existence of God. Aquinas, despite his attention to the problems involved in speaking of the nature of God, appears to have assumed that the question of his existence was essentially akin to that of some merely physical object. Put another way, he supposed that, for us at least, "God exists" must be a merely factual and contingent claim. And his influence and example have been such that since his time even apparently sophisticated philosophers have continued to treat the matter in this same way. They have been content to debate the truth or falsity of this claim or, especially of late, the adequacy of the evidence for and against it. It is, however, now clear that both these charges require something more. They can be answered only by laying bare the distinctive logic of this claim. Or rather, as we shall see, only by laying bare that of its properly religious counterpart. They are not answered by an ordinary demonstration of its truth or by any mere assemblage of evidence. Their challenge is one which can be met only by a clarification of the nature and logic of this and similar claims.

But the modernity and sophistication of these charges is only a part of their story. Equally important, they grow out of and reflect a philosophical tradition which, at least in the Anglo-Saxon world, has always been incipiently empiricist and even positivistic. More specifically, they reflect a number of restrictive and doubtful dogmas concerning the functions of language. Indeed, they are perhaps best seen as expressions of these dogmas. But this is not said in order to make the easy point that these charges therefore beg the real issue. Rather it is to underscore their connection with our philosophical tradition and to make the point that they will not be fully answered until the dogmas of that tradition have themselves been called into question.

All this can be put more positively. The real objection to the earlier positivist charge of Ayer and his followers was that it employed the term "meaningless" in an invidious and, ultimately, purely technical sense. [1] A crude device, it was useful in condemning religious utterances but quite worthless as a means of discovering the real nature and complexity of such utterances or, indeed, of belief itself. Similarly, most of the historic discussions of the existence of God seem to have been intended to establish or dispute a given claim rather than to uncover its logic and significance; unless, that is, with certain moderns, we read the historic "proofs" as explications of belief. In this sense both encounters have been less enlightening than they might have been. No doubt the present charges might be treated in much the same way but they also invite another and more fruitful approach. They provide an occasion for exploring the various uses of genuinely religious utterances. They can be an incentive to discover the various kinds of meaning such utterances actually have. They can be a stimulus to articulate the logic and nature of the real foundations of belief. This is their real value and this is how they should be treated.

In recent years there have been many attempts to answer or at least speak to these charges. Mr. John Hick has insisted upon eschatological verification as a possible way of meeting the unfalsifiability charge. [2] Other philosophers have pointed to inconsistencies in the demand that beliefs be falsifiable. [3] Still others, as already suggested, have concluded that the equating of "meaningful" with "falsifiable" is itself invidious and prejudicial. [4] Mr. R. M. Hare has suggested that religious beliefs or

---

[1] As much is often made of the changes between the first and subsequent editions of A. J. Ayer's *Language, Truth and Logic* it is perhaps worth pointing out that this objection applies to the latter no less than to the former.

[2] John Hick, *Faith and Knowledge* (Ithaca, N.Y., Cornell University Press, 1957), pp. 155-161.

[3] Cf., for example, George I. Mavrodes, "God and Verification", *Canadian Journal of Theology*, X, No. 3 (July, 1964).

[4] Cf., e.g., Frederick Ferré, *Language, Logic and God* (London, Eyre & Spottiswoode, 1962), especially pp. 42-66.

"bliks" are ostensibly referential, that they do indeed effect conduct but that they are, however, never subject to falsification. [5] Professor Braithwaite has surrendered the factual content of religious belief and represents it as primarly a helpful and necessary guide to right attitudes and actions. [6] Professor I. T. Ramsey has emphasized the factual or empirical element within such belief, but at the same time points out how such claims go beyond the merely empirical, at least in the obvious sense of that term. [7] And, like many contemporary writers, he agrees that no empirical evidence could count for or against properly religious claims. [8]

It is scarcely too much to say that none of the above have completely answered either of these charges; certainly they have not wrung all the juice from these particular lemons. Some have been content to take the short road with their adversaries. Generally speaking, however, most have fallen prey to one or more of the many shortcomings characteristic of much recent work in this field. They have failed to question the philosophical assumptions underlying these charges. They have accepted the conception of religion as consisting primarily in assent to a set of factual propositions. They have adopted the critics' purported examples of religious utterances and, equally important, their seriously misleading interpretation of these utterances. They have neglected the precise form of the believer's claims, disregarded the various contexts within which they are used and remained oblivious to the variety of senses in which they are actually employed. In short, they have not treated religion and its distinctive utterances upon anything like their own terms.

[5] R. M. Hare in "Theology and Falsification", *New Essays in Philosophical Theology*, ed. A. G. N. Flew and Alasdair MacIntyre (London, S.C.M. Press, 1955), pp. 99–103.
[6] R. B. Braithwaite, *An Empiricist's View of the Nature of Religious Belief* (Cambridge, Cambridge University Press, 1955).
[7] I. T. Ramsey, *Religious Language* (London, S.C.M. Press, 1957) esp. pp. 49–89. Cf. also I. T. Ramsey, *Models and Mystery* (London, Oxford University Press, 1964).
[8] Smart, Wisdom and Findlay have also produced important and influential discussions of the question of the existence of God. However, these discussions treat that existence as merely factual and contingent. They are therefore more an expression of our second charge than an answer to it.

These failings are particularly evident in recent discussions of the existence of God. Here especially the defenders of religion have tended to follow its critics. In effect, they have ascribed the utterance "God exists" to the believer and, equally important, they have interpreted this as a single and, again, a simple, factual but contingent claim. This is, however, quite unjustified. It is not simply that this particular utterance is vitiated by a radical logical impropriety. The fact is that the believer scarcely ever employs this utterance and, when he does so, intends it in a sense very different from that which the critic imagines. Hence the ascription of this form burdens the believer with a claim which quite misrepresents his actual position. In fact, this utterance is so a-typical of religious language, so far from what the believer can actually intend, that one can only wonder that it is still bandied about at a time when there is so much emphasis upon actual use.

Obviously any work which hopes to answer these charges must take a much firmer line. It must reject the prejudice that empirical generalizations constitute a prototype or norm of proper discourse and it must refuse any model which reflects, however surreptitiously, this assumption. It must see religion as an interpretative activity related to and affecting the whole life of man. It must use as examples, not the utterances which philosophers have traditionally ascribed to believers, but rather those which believers themselves naturally employ. It must reject the assumption that such utterances have and can have but a single meaning which can be determined independently of the context in which they occur. It must refuse to accept any positivist or quasi-positivist theory or test of meaning. It must undertake a careful analysis of the principal contexts in which these utterances are employed and thus distinguish their various key senses. And it must do so not in the light of traditional or current theories about how language ought to function, but rather as an open and unprejudiced attempt to chart and understand its actual uses. The patient cataloguing of actual practice is the proper alternative to the imposition of *a priori* and perhaps largely unconscious theories. Language behaves in the various ways men make it behave; this is not the last thing to be said on the subject but it is certainly the first.

Our own approach is very direct and simple. This study does not work from or even towards any general theory of how language does or ought to function. Instead, it simply attempts to provide an accurate description of the three principal uses of certain characteristic religious utterances. Naturally there will be no attempt to prove the truth of these utterances or, except in the formal sense, to spell out their content. The aim is simply to discover the various things the believer intends and in this way to determine whether his utterances and belief are open to the charges before us. It is only after we have discovered the various senses of a particular utterance that we can ask which are unfalsifiable and in what sense. So, too, it is only after we have discovered the real logic of the foundation of his belief that we can decide concerning the charge that it is undemonstrated and indemonstrable.

We are concerned to discover the logic of the various uses of genuinely religious utterances and shall work throughout with two genuine and typical examples of this class. The familiar "God is love" already mentioned is quite in order and will be our first example. But, as already suggested, the equally familiar "God exists" is open to grave suspicion. Philosophers do indeed discuss this claim but, quite rightly, believers scarcely ever use this form. Instead, with the Apostles' Creed, they say, "I believe in God". We shall therefore take this as our second example. [9] At least so far as our present purposes are concerned, this utterance is essentially akin to the first.

In our discussion of these examples we shall deliberately emphasize the principal contexts in which they are actually employed. This is not simply a reaction to those who treat utterances as having meaning in and of themselves. Essentially it is because these contexts provide the simplest and most reliable clue to the different uses of such utterances, and hence to the various senses in terms of which we hope to answer these charges.

[9] These examples reflect actual use but, equally important, they also raise the crucial questions. This is underscored, for example, by Flew's presentation of the falsification issue. "What would have to occur or to have occurred to constitute for you a disproof of the love of, or of the existence of, God?" A. G. N. Flew, "Theology and Falsification", *New Essays in Philosophical Theology*, p. 99.

In order to set forth more clearly the uses of religious utterances, we shall begin with a model or claim having the same complex relation to scientific activity as our own examples have to religious belief and practice. The philosophical critics of science have provided many instances of such claims but we shall content ourselves with the simple and obvious "The world has an order". The choice of a model from this particular area has many reasons, some of which are quite obvious. Though the scientists have not explicitly answered their critics, their actual use of this and similar statements provides the basis for an answer to the charges before us. Further, these charges rest ultimately upon certain traditional and restrictive theories about the way in which words and, derivatively, utterances can function. It seems best therefore to begin with a model from another realm, a model which actually functions in a way not allowed by these theories. When its behaviour has been charted we shall then be in a better position to proceed to the various uses of our examples and, hence, of religious utterances as such.

Both our model and our examples have the same three principal uses. These can be described respectively as the *assertional*, the *self-instructional* and, for want of a better term, the *ontological-linguistic* use or sense. The use of both "use" and "sense" is deliberate, though the distinction is not absolute. Generally speaking, the former will stand for the believer's actual use or employment of the utterance and the latter for the sense or meaning which he intends in and by that use.

The first and second of these uses occur within a discipline while the third is, in an important sense, outside of and prior to it. Hence the last is, properly speaking, a *meta*-use. To be more precise, it is a *meta*-scientific or, as the case may be, a *meta*-religious use. Nothing hangs upon this purely classificatory device but it may prove helpful to mark off the third use in this way.

The three different types of uses distinguished above are closely linked to two different uses of the key or operative concept of the utterance in question. These we shall describe as the *determinate* and the *heuristic* use or sense and indicate as, for example, love(m) [or (n) or (o)] and love (X), respectively. The ordinary letters, chosen from the middle of the alphabet, indicate that the concept is being used to stand for one or other of a set of determinate and specifiable values. The X, borrowed from simple algebra, indicates that it is being used in an entirely different way; indeed, this letter has been capitalized simply in order to underscore this difference. In this case the speaker knows that the concept has a value but he does not know, and does not profess to know, precisely what this value is; in fact, he is using the term to stand in for this value until it can be discovered. It goes without saying that in all cases both the various senses of the term and the different uses of the utterance reflect the intention of the speaker and, behind this, the context of his utterance.

Despite these perhaps distracting details the underlying strategy of this investigation is extremely simple. It employs our scientific model to help distinguish the three principal uses of religious utterances and, upon the basis of these uses, attempts to answer the charges before us.

The course of our overall argument is both obvious and simple. The second chapter describes the three senses in which the scientist uses our model, and indicates briefly the way in which this utterance and his discipline may be cleared of charges precisely similar to those with which we are here concerned. The third chapter deals specifically with the "unfalsifiable and vacuous" charge: it considers the believer's three typical uses of each of our religious examples and indicates the extent to which each of these is open to this charge. The fourth chapter deals with the "undemonstrated and indemonstrable" charge: it concentrates upon the believer's first and, particularly, his third use of each of these utterances and, concentrating upon the distinctive nature of the latter use, exposes the confusions underlying this charge. The fifth chapter offers certain concluding remarks concerning the conception of religious belief presupposed by these answers.

The reader is now perhaps in a better position to appreciate the importance of concentrating upon the actual utterances of religious believers. In particular, he can perhaps better appreciate the importance of using the believer's utterance "I believe in God" rather than the philosophers' traditional "God exists". Perhaps largely because of its linguistic form, the latter has been treated as a simple factual claim and the variety of its uses entirely neglected. Even to the unpracticed eye the believer's utterance is, of course, more rich and complex. It contains two separate layers, a performative or declarative aspect expressed in "I believe..." and an assertional aspect or element which may be indicated with the words "... that there is a God". (This is not altogether adequate but will perhaps do for the moment.) The first layer shapes the second, making each use of the utterance quite different from "God exists" as traditionally conceived. This is true even of the third or *meta*-religious use which, though it performs the task traditionally assigned to the philosophers' "God exists", does so in an entirely different way. The believer's utterance is therefore quite distinct from the simple theistic thesis which philosophers traditionally ascribe to religious believers. Perhaps the traditional form can be convicted of the charges before us. It is our hope that by examining the utterances which believers actually employ, and by distinguishing their various uses, we can answer these charges and even expose some of the misapprehensions upon which they rest.

We have already suggested that these charges reflect certain of the characteristic dogmas of our philosophical tradition and that they can be answered finally only by bringing these dogmas into question. Both of these suggestions require further brief comment. Most of these dogmas are familiar in one form or another: words and utterances have meaning *per se;* this meaning can be discovered independently of context; the grammatical form of an utterance is a reliable guide to its real nature and logic; terms can be used only in a determinate or specifiable sense; utterances are genuine statements only if their terms are so used; statements are meaningful only if they are falsifiable; all statements are either analytic or synthetic; no factual claim can be more than contingently true. It might be thought that nothing less than a detailed, point by point refutation of these claims would suffice. In fact, this would amount only to showing the possibility of some alternative view. These are *a priori* theories and should be met not with rival theories but with clear counter-instances. The proper way to refute these restrictive dogmas is by the production of instances in which language actually functions in ways which they do not allow.

Our earlier account of this work as an attempt to answer certain charges against religious belief requires one minor qualification. This puts the matter too simply and is perhaps open to unnecessary misunderstanding. It is no part of our purpose to defend the confused believer against the hard-headed critic. Our underlying concern is rather to clarify the nature of religious belief. And there can be little doubt that such clarification is needed. Believers have often been bemused and even bullied by their philosophical critics into accepting a quite misleading and inaccurate account of the nature of belief. This, indeed, is why so many simply assume that their claims are unfalsifiable and that their belief is without any rational foundation. But whatever their conscious account, their utterances are still largely innocent of such theory and a careful examination of their various uses should reveal the fundamental and essential character of religious belief.

A final word concerning the use of a model from the realm of science. This choice has not been made with any thought of attempting to commend religion and its utterances by comparing it with a currently prestigious discipline and its claims. Nor has it been made simply for the obvious reasons already given. The real grounds of this choice are in fact much more fundamental and revealing. Between religion and science there are indeed certain obvious and important differences [10] and the present fashion is to concentrate almost entirely upon them. But the fact remains that these two or, more accurately, Christianity and science form

[10] For example, religion involves the adoption of certain attitudes and courses of action whereas, generally speaking, pure science does not. Religion tends to concentrate upon rare and presumably unrepeatable events while science deliberately restricts itself to public and repeatable ones. Religion attempts to see events as an expression of the fundamental reality behind the world and so aims at explanation in a truly radical sense; science consciously restricts itself to what have historically been called efficient causes and so settles for the description as opposed to the explanation of events. These differences are important but they do not tell against our claim that Christianity and science are both essentially interpretative activities and that in this they are therefore fundamentally similar.

a real historical continuum. And this is no mere accident of history. Though each has its own distinctive interests and concerns, they share a common basic structure and they reflect the same fundamental orientation and approach. Both are born of the same desire to understand the nature of reality and both pursue this quest in accordance with the same basic laws of the human understanding. Both are, in fact, expressions of the human drive to achieve understanding and can be adequately grasped only as such. [11] That there actually is such a similarity will, we hope, emerge in the course of our investigation. For the moment it is perhaps sufficient to say that this similarity, together with the fact that we now have a better understanding of the logic of scientific discourse, is the real reason why we have chosen a model from science to illuminate the logic of religious belief and its claims.

---

[11] One of the first of the modern thinkers to insist upon the essential continuity of religion and science was, of course, the late Dr. A. N. Whitehead; see, for example, *Science and the Modern World*, chap. I, "The Origins of Modern Science". Another important figure in this connection was the late Michael Foster, who was particularly concerned with the Judaic-Christian tradition as an historical source of modern science; see, especially, "The Christian Doctrine of Creation and the Rise of Modern Natural Science", *Mind*, XLIII, N.S., pp. 446–468 and "Christian Theology and Modern Science of Nature", *Mind*, XLIV, N.S., pp. 439–466 and XLV, N.S., pp. 1-27.

II

A MODEL FROM SCIENCE

Both our aim and strategy have already been indicated. We hope to answer two current charges against religion with the help of a distinction between the three main uses of typically religious utterances. The present chapter is a first step toward this goal. It charts and describes the corresponding uses of a model from science and, on the basis of these distinctions, proceeds to show how this discipline is to be defended against precisely similar charges.

There are many reasons for choosing a model from this particular realm in addition to those mentioned at the end of the last chapter. As previously noted, science has been subject to charges very similar to those now standing against religion. That this is perhaps not so obvious in the case of the first or unfalsifiability charge is itself suggestive and revealing. The point that certain of the scientists' crucial utterances are not open to any final falsification has already been made by a number of philosophers including, for example, Warnock [1] and, less clearly, Waismann. [2]

---

[1] G. J. Warnock, "Every Event Has a Cause", *Logic and Language* (Second Series), ed. A.G.N. Flew (New York, Philosophical Library, 1953), esp. pp. 109 f.
[2] Friedrich Waismann, "Verifiability", *Logic and Language* (First Series) ed. A.G.N. Flew (New York, Philosophical Library), 1951, esp. pp. 131–37. The kind of utterance with which we are here particularly concerned is perhaps best described as *meta*-scientific but it is worth noting the strict line taken by Popper, for example, concerning scientific theories as such. "One can sum up all this by saying that *falsifiability, or refutability, is the criterion of the scientific status of a theory*." Karl Popper, "Philosophy of Science: A. Personal Report", *British Philosophy in the Mid-Century*, ed. C.A. Mace (London, Allen & Unwin, 1957), p. 160.

That this was neither intended nor accepted as a charge is perhaps not surprising. No one is any longer particularly concerned to discredit science. Philosophers are now much more aware that language has a variety of functions and, connected with this, many are now much less inclined to identify unfalsifiability and meaninglessness. These considerations help to explain why this point was not seen as a real objection to science, but this shift in perspective is really irrelevant to our present concern. Charge or observation, this claim is still essentially similar to the first of the current charges against religion and there is good reason to think that the answers to both are fundamentally alike.

The scientific counterpart of the second charge is of course much more familiar and straightforward. From the time of Hume until the present, philosophers have continued to urge his point against the inductive sciences. Even Bertrand Russell, at least in *The Problems of Philosophy*, [3] suggests that science is based upon the universality of causal connection interpreted as a simply contingent fact. Similar claims have been made by others whose names are much less celebrated but the classic expression is still that of Hume. He claimed that science rested upon certain assumptions concerning the nature of the world. In particular, he claimed that it rested upon the belief that the future will resemble the past [4] and, elsewhere, and perhaps less explicitly, that every event has a cause. [5] He held that science presupposed the truth of these claims and that it necessarily awaited their demonstration. And he further held that these assumptions had not been and, at least so far as he could see, could not be demonstrated. In short, and in our own words, he held that the foundations of science were undemonstrated and indemonstrable.

It is perhaps worth adding that the attack against science resembles that against religion even in certain important matters of detail. This is particularly so in respect of the second charge. In this case both sets of critics have regularly provided the claims

---

[3] Bertrand Russell, *The Problems of Philosophy*, Chap. VI.
[4] Hume, *An Enquiry Concerning Human Understanding*, § IV.
[5] Hume, *Treatise of Human Nature*, Bk. I, Pt. III, § iii. Cf. also *An Enquiry Concerning Human Understanding*, § VII.

for which they hold their victims accountable and, not content with this, have insisted upon interpreting these in their own particular way, *viz.*, as merely contingent factual claims. Deliberately or not, they have made their charge seem plausible by the simple expedient of neglecting the various contexts and the variety of uses in which these utterances are actually employed.

The second obvious reason for this particular choice has also been suggested. Although the scientists have scarcely bothered to answer these charges, the fact remains that their various uses of certain characteristic utterances clearly provides the basis for such an answer. These uses reveal how the scientists would answer these charges if they thought it worthwhile to do so. The examination of these uses in the case of our model should therefore help us to recognize the parallel uses of our own examples and, ultimately, to spell out the answer to the corresponding charges against religion.

In fact, there is another and closely connected reason for beginning in this way. As already suggested, both these charges against religion rest ultimately upon certain traditional and restrictive theories about the way in which words and, derivatively, utterances can function. In fact, certain uses of our model provide clear counter-instances of these theories. Their examination should therefore help us escape these theories and, by the same token, grasp the various ways in which religious utterances are actually used. However, before proceeding in this direction it will be helpful to examine Hume's charge more closely. Any detailed criticism is plainly out of the question but it should be possible to indicate briefly where it went wrong and how it is mistaken.

Any evaluation of Hume's views on this subject will depend in large measure upon one's assessment of his underlying motive and about this, unfortunately, it is difficult to be certain. His purpose may have been to make the point that science could not be justified by empirical generalizations and hence not in the way his contemporaries imagined. This is supported by the fact that his examples appear to be at least of the kind to which they appealed most frequently. It also helps to explain the otherwise perplexing fact that he was apparently prepared to go to inordinate lengths to press a charge which, on his own showing, is fundamentally unanswerable. If this is so, his point is perfectly sound and, indeed, important. But it seems more likely that his real purpose was to embarrass science just as, in other writings, he attempted to embarrass religion. This is suggested by his repeated claim that in the nature of the case the foundations of science do not admit of any kind of demonstration. It is also suggested by the overall tone of his remarks, a tone which seems intended to convey the impression that he had caught science in a kind of stymie move from which it could not possibly escape. If this was indeed his purpose then his remarks are much more obviously open to question. The fault is not always with the accused and it is at least odd to charge science with lacking the kind of foundation which, on one's own showing, it could not possibly possess. Indeed, if matters are precisely as Hume alleges, the real trouble is not with science but with his charge or, at least, with the particular manner in which it is formulated.

One thing is, however, clear. For whatever reason, Hume accepted an inaccurate and even fundamentally misleading conception of science. He sees it as consisting simply of a number of empirical generalizations. Quite naturally, therefore, he supposes that the real problem is to justify our belief or confidence in its conclusions. In fact, he had no conception of science as an ongoing interpretative activity or orientation, nor any grasp of the fact that the problem was to justify it thus conceived. This appears to be the real source of the ambiguity which pervades his treatment of this whole question.

Hume's other main assumption is closely connected with this. Though he rejects the then current view that the world was specially designed to conform to human intelligence he did hold that science was possible only if this was indeed a certain kind of world. In short, he accepted the "happy accident" theory of science in its essential form. Naturally therefore, he supposed that it could be justified only if it could be shown that this was in fact so. He was searching for an assurance that the world was a certain way. He was looking for a guarantee that it actually possessed some feature or quality which it might conceivably lack.

All this is borne out by the way in which Hume interprets his own examples. He sees these claims as stating simple and contingent matters of fact, as asserting something about the world which, while perhaps true, might nevertheless be false. In short, and however implausibly, he believed that science could be justified only by the prior establishment of certain pseudo-scientific or perhaps metaphysical claims. In the final analysis it was this which prompted him to regard his own examples as factual assertions, to suppose that they could be established only by means of empirical investigation, and to conclude that, since this was clearly impossible, science itself could never be properly justified. By the same token, it was this fundamental assumption which restricted his conception as to what might serve as a possible answer to his own challenge.

There is, of course, no doubt that Hume's examples, at least as he interpreted them, are undemonstrated and indemonstrable. We do not know that the future will actually resemble the past. Nor do we know that there always has been and always will be a cause for every event. Such claims are unknown and unknowable in principle and in fact. And if we could establish them it would necessarily be by means of empirical investigation and hence in a way which begs the question it presumes to settle. Science cannot be justified in this way and Hume was quite right in his claim that his particular demands could not be answered. But the argument which establishes this also shows that the foundation of science could not possibly be some merely contingent matter of fact. That Hume failed to draw this obvious conclusion may have a psychological or even pedagogical explanation. Ultimately, however, it seems to stem from the fact that he mistook the nature of science and hence the real character of its foundation.

It is perhaps worth adding that though he was unable to demonstrate the foundations of science Hume seems to have accepted its conclusions and to have held that men were fundamentally right in doing so. Here, of course, he was rescued by his familiar conception of habit. His critics have pointed out that this is a merely psychological solution which does not really answer the question at issue. It is, however, more relevant to remark that, perhaps not surprisingly, this justification reflects precisely the same kind of blind fideism which Hume finds in his own version of the Christian religion. [6] That this account of the foundations of science is quite mistaken will emerge from a consideration of the various uses of our model.

1

The scientist has three quite distinct uses for utterances like our model, "The world has an order": when he has just discovered a particular order, when some strange event has challenged his familiar conceptions and, finally, when he is attempting to meet the philosophers' challenge to defend the assumptions of his discipline. The next step is to describe the distinctive sense or meaning of each of these typical uses.

Imagine a scientist who has finally discovered a causal link between A and B. He has unearthed a connection between two types of events and later will spell it out in detail. He will in fact describe it as fully and accurately as possible. But for the moment his concern is simply to report or announce his discovery. He can do this in a number of ways: "There was a connection after all'; "Yes, I have discovered the law"; or, in a more expansive mood, "The world has an order". He means, of course, a particular connection, a particular law and, equally, a particular order.

This use of "order" is quite clear from both the context and the suggested alternative formulations. The scientist has discovered a particular order or uniformity and wishes to report this fact. Hence "order" is simply shorthand for a particular or determinate order, an order which he could produce or specify upon demand. This is the determinate sense or use of the term and can be marked as order(m).

Leaving aside for the moment the relatively complicated question of the existence of such orders (Does anyone now wish to assert the existence of Newtonian gravity?), the nature of this

---

[6] Hume, *An Enquiry Concerning Human Understanding*, § X.

utterance seems quite clear. It is intended as a factual claim on all fours with "There is a cat in the next room", "There is a tree on the lower campus", etc. It asserts a state of affairs (that A is the cause of B) and can be falsified by a single counter-instance (a case where B is not preceded by A). This is the assertional use of the utterance and can be expressed as "The world has order(m)". Though this is one of the commonest uses of this utterance, it is not by any manner the most interesting. Further, since it is the result of scientific investigation, it cannot possibly be its foundation.

But this same utterance also appears in another and perhaps more revealing context. Imagine that our scientist has failed to discover the suspected causal connection; imagine even that he has encountered evidence which tells decisively against conceptions he has long held. He could, of course, give up in despair; he could decide that there was no hope of making sense of all the evidence before him. Alternatively, he could recall his scientific commitment to see every single part as coherent with the whole. In that event he might well steady himself with the remark "Everything must fit together"; "The universe is a single whole"; or, equally appropriate, "The world has an order".

It is, of course, clear that in this case the scientist is no longer using the word "order" as shorthand for some determinate or specifiable regularity. Again, it is equally clear that he does not intend his utterance in anything like its earlier sense. Indeed, in the present context, he need not intend a claim about the world at all. He is rather telling himself to treat every event as part of the world; to see all phenomena, however strange, as falling within its order. Of course, he is not enjoining himself to force this event into some conception he already has. Instead, he is instructing himself to get on with the job of formulating a conception having room for this event. Again, he is using "order" not to stand for this or that particular order but simply for order as such. He is using it in the sense of "form", "shape" or "way". He is using it in its heuristic sense and this we can mark as order (X).

It is important not to be misled by the linguistic form of "The world has an order". Here it is not a claim about the world but rather a pledge or vow which the scientist is taking. It is his self-command to get on with the job, to continue in the scientific enterprise. This is the self-instructional use and can be expressed as "Treat every single event as relevant to the proper determination of the world's order(X)" or, more briefly, "Treat all events as part of the world's order(X)".

It is perhaps worth noting that this use can be given another and equally valid formulation. It can in fact be expressed as "In this context understand 'order' in its heuristic sense". This is, significantly, an equivalent form of self-instruction.

The description of this use of "order" as heuristic may require some comment and explanation. It is of course clear that it is not here used in anything like its ordinary sense. As already seen, the intended meaning of this use of the utterance can be expressed in terms of the use of the word or, for that matter, without even mentioning it. It is employed because of circumstances which would ordinarily prompt most men to think instead of its opposite. Finally, the scientist who uses it cannot say or even pretend to be able to say precisely what, in the ordinary sense, he means by it; he cannot now produce or specify that determinate order which the world actually has. But there is another sense of "meaning" [7] according to which he knows perfectly well what he means. "Order" is his name for the world's "form", "shape" or "way". It is his marker for "the way the world is, however that may prove to be". This might prompt a contemporary philosopher to say that this term has a use but no meaning. But this would neglect a very important element in the situation. Though the scientist cannot now specify the determinate meaning of "order" he knows that it does in fact have such a meaning. He even knows where it is to be found and precisely how it is to be determined. And he uses this term to stand in for that meaning until it has been

---

[7] This seems to be at least close to one of the senses of "meaning" which Wittgenstein was concerned to uncover. Cf., for example, "For a *large* class of cases – though not for all – in which we employ the word "meaning" it can be defined thus: the meaning of a word is its use in the language. And the *meaning* of a name is sometimes explained by pointing to its bearer." Wittgenstein, *Philosophical Investigations,* transl. G. E. Anscombe (Basil Blackwell, 1953), Pt. I, 43.

finally determined. This is what is intended by describing this as its heuristic use.

It is of course true that words are most frequently used in their determinate sense; this no doubt explains the *prima facie* plausibility of what has recently been called the picture theory of language. But clearly they are sometimes successfully and properly used even when we are quite unable to specify what is ordinarily called their meaning. In such situations they are used not like a picture but like a mirror; not to present a fixed and constant image but rather to reflect and copy that upon which they are directed. They are used not in their determinate but in another and more fundamental sense. This is perhaps most obvious in the case of the variable in a simple algebraic equation. Before the student can specify the determinate meaning of X, before he can even begin to solve the equation, he must first grasp the meaning of this term in this other sense; before he can set out to discover its numerical value he must first know that it stands for some such value. He must know that this value is determined entirely by the equation in which it occurs and that it is being used to stand in for that value until it has been discovered. He must read it as a mirror rather than as a picture. What we call algebraic equations are possible because terms can function in this way. Similarly, their ordinary language counterparts are possible because, traditional dogmas notwithstanding, we can and sometimes do use certain terms in their heuristic sense.

The self-instructional use of this utterance, like the heuristic use of "order", is obviously important for science. It characterizes or, better, constitutes an approach as scientific. The first rule in the game of science is that all events must be treated as part of the whole. The scientist's self-instructional use of his utterance is his rehearsal of this primary rule; it is his explicit undertaking to treat all events in this way. It is his agreement to be bound by the rules of this particular game. Of course any individual scientist might in fact forsake this rule but he cannot do so as a scientist. In this role he is bound to treat all events as part of the whole. To do otherwise would be contrary to his fundamental resolve and commitment. To be a scientist is not to impose some *a priori* conception of order upon the world; it is rather to undertake to see the world as a single, coherent whole. It is to agree that all the various events of the world shall inform and determine our understanding of its order.

It is worth noting that the other familiar assumptions of science can also be used in this same self-instructional sense. Their linguistic form notwithstanding, "Every event has a cause" and "The future will resemble the past" need not be intended as factual claims. The first need not be a prediction that every event will, in fact, have a cause, and the second need not be an assertion of the continuity of world history. In the situation described they would in fact be intended quite differently. They would be resolutions; the first to treat every event as though it had a cause, the second to treat all future events as integral with those of the past. In short, both would be resolves to treat experience in a certain way.

Both of the preceding uses occur within scientific activity proper, or at least on its immediate borders. But the scientist has another and very different use for his utterance. This is the one with which he meets the philosophers' challenge to state and defend the assumptions of his discipline. This use falls outside scientific activity proper and is therefore, strictly, a *meta*-use. Actual instances are notoriously and, perhaps, significantly rare but the use is nevertheless interesting and highly instructive. The distinctive nature of this use can be brought out by comparing it with the answer which the philosophers expect and require the scientist to give.

Since the time of Hume philosophers have been prone to assume that science can be justified only by showing that this is indeed a certain kind of world. They have required a demonstration or, at the very least, a reasonable assurance that the world was a certain way; for example, that it had an objective pattern, that it was sufficiently orderly, that it had the requisite degree of simplicity, that it was suitably geared to the human mind, etc. They have required an assurance concerning what was essentially a contingent matter of fact. That indeed is why they have talked as though science depended upon the world's possession of some quality or feature which it might conceivably lack. This is what lies behind Hume's preoccupation with apparently factual claims and his apparent attempt to justify science in this way.

It is, of course, clear that the scientist who accepts this challenge on its own terms commits himself to some such claim about the world. Such a scientist would therefore use our utterance to say something essentially similar to that which he says in the first situation; similar, but of course, much more general. He would, in fact, intended it in what is best called its "metaphysical" sense. Of course it is precisely this sense which the scientist seeks and must seek to avoid.

Objections to the alleged metaphysical justification of science, and hence to this particular use, are of course familiar and notorious. It is not simply that such generalizations can never be adequately established and are therefore always open to doubt. More to the point, they cannot serve as the foundations of science for the simple reason that they must themselves be the product of science. As Hume pointed out, they presuppose what they purport to establish. Those who continue to demand a metaphysical justification for science should recall Hume's proof that such demonstration is logically impossible. [8]

Of course this means that the scientist who is using our model to justify his discipline cannot employ the term "order" in its determinate sense. He cannot now use it to make an empirical or even metaphysical assertion about the world. But it would be wrong to conclude that he cannot employ the term "order" at all or that he cannot significantly apply it to the world. Whether such use and application is possible is the crucial question and it is not to be settled by mere *a priori* prejudice or the acceptance of familiar theories about the way in which language ought to function.

The standard Humean objection shows only the impossibility of a metaphysical justification for science, but there is another objection which points to the justification which the scientist actually intends. The underlying difficulty with the metaphysical

[8] Hume, *An Enquiry Concerning Human Understanding*, § VII. Cf. also *Treatise of Human Nature*, Bk. I, Pt. III, § iii.

one is that it assumes an essentially pretentious and unrealistic account of the insight or understanding afforded by science and, as a result, accounts for the intelligibility of the world in terms of what is essentially a happy accident. In fact, science does not require that the world have this shape or that. It requires only that it have some shape or other. It requires only that the world have order in the pristine or, better, the heuristic sense of that term. And this it cannot lack. Science is not contingent upon some happy accident. Its only condition is one which could not possibly be absent.

The difference between these two rival accounts can be put very simply. The Humean philosopher supposes that science is possible only if the world has a pattern or, failing that, at least a minimal degree of orderliness. The scientist knows that it is possible provided only that the events and objects of the world exist in some determinate relation to one another. He knows that the condition of the world being an object for science is in fact identical with that of it being a world or, indeed, anything at all.

Imagine that you are playing the game of pick-up sticks. The sticks have been spilled upon the table and you are about to begin picking them up one by one without, of course, moving any other. Recalling their original symmetrical arrangement, you are perhaps inclined to say that they are now disordered; indeed, you may even hold that this disorder is a condition of the game. Imagine, however, that, as you are about to touch the first stick, a voice announces that the rules have been changed and that now the game is simply to describe the spatial relations existing between the various sticks. Suddenly the pile takes on a new appearance; as we ordinarily say, it *assumes* an order. No longer a merely chaotic pile, it is now seen as a bundle having precise and determinate internal relations. It is seen as something having an order which, though yet unknown, is in fact knowable. It is this order, together of course with the noticing of this order, which makes the pile an object for science. In certain cases we may fail to notice the order; there may even be cases in which there would be no point in our doing so. But this order is always there; indeed, it could not possibly be absent. Every pile must always have order in this sense and so is always open to scientific description. Similarly the world must also possess order in this sense and so is necessarily a possible object for science. This means that obvious pattern or evident orderliness is not a condition of science. This is the "happy accident" theory which makes it rest upon a bet which can never be justified. What makes science possible is just the fact that at every moment the world does and must exist in some particular way. It is this fact which is the ground and guarantee of the world's intelligibility. That the world has and must have some shape or other is the fact to which the scientist wishes to call attention. In the face of his Humean critic it is all he wishes and, more important, all he needs to say.

There is, of course, an obvious and familiar objection to this account of the conditions of science. Many philosophers refuse to allow that science really explains anything but they are greatly, and perhaps naturally, impressed by its remarkable powers of prediction. This they interpret as evidence that the world does indeed have the requisite degree of simplicity and that the hypothesis upon which the description is based must itself be a correct description of that part of the world with which it is concerned. But, quite apart from the fact that it places too much emphasis upon the merely predictive aspect of science, there are other serious difficulties in this objection. The argument from the success of the prediction to the truth of the underlying conception is one from consequent to antecedent and, as such, is and must always be fallacious. Further, as history fully demonstrates, it is possible to achieve even extreme success in prediction upon the basis of what have subsequently proven to be obviously inadequate hypotheses and conceptions. The capacity of science to predict may tell us something of the nature of the operation of the human mind, but it cannot be evidence for either the literal veracity of particular conceptions or the essential simplicity of the world.

We are perhaps now in a better position to understand the sense in which the scientist uses the term "order" when attempting to answer his critic. It is, of course, clear that he does not and need not use it as shorthand for a particular order which, as in his determinate use of this term, he might now conceivably specify.

Nor, again, is he using it to stand for an obvious or recognizable pattern. Indeed, he is not using it in either of these ordinary and familiar senses. Instead, he is using it in its generic sense of "form", "shape" or "way". He is using it as a stand-in or name for the actual character of the world, whatever that should prove to be. This, too, is the heuristic use of the term and can be marked as order(X).

This particular use has already been compared to both a mirror and the variable in a simple algebraic equation. Both figures suggest its central and distinguishing feature. Here "order" is not simply what we have learned to call an open-textured concept. It is not simply that its lines are somewhat shifting and blurred. Its use here is in fact quite different from the ordinary one. In this case the scientist is not using it as a determinate conception or implicit description which he might project, however tentatively, upon the world. It does not stand for some fully developed conception he already has. Instead, it is a name or token the meaning of which, he agrees, is to be determined finally and entirely by the world. It is his tentative marker for something which he knows to exist but which he cannot yet adequately specify.

It is perhaps worth noting that even in this context "order" does have a meaning in the ordinary sense of that term. At least it does if terms of themselves can have meaning. This is true even if the world is in fact in a constant state of evolution and change. And the scientist knows that it has such a meaning; he even knows the rules he must follow if he is to discover it. But he also knows that at this point in his endeavours he cannot spell out or provide this meaning. He cannot therefore be using "order" in its ordinary or determinate sense.

We should now better understand the precise sense in which the scientist here uses his entire utterance. It is, of course, no longer a piece of self-instruction. Roughly, and as its form suggests, it is a statement about the world. More precisely, it is a taking note of or a calling attention to a fact about the world. It is an assertion that the world does have an order; though not, of course, as in the first use, that it has this order or that. Here the same words are used to assert something entirely different. They are employed to call attention to the fact that the world has some one particular order, shape or form. Put linguistically, they are used to express the scientist's account of the connection between the concepts "world" and "order". When he so uses our model to justify his work the scientist is employing it in its ontological-linguistic sense. This we can express as "The world has order(X)".

This use can be specified more precisely. The scientist is pointing out that the world has and must have some one shape or way. He is not describing the character of the world but claiming that it must have some character. He is not saying that the world has some particular order but calling attention to the much more fundamental and primary fact that it must have some particular order or other.

The scientist's position in this matter is quite different from another which it superficially resembles. He is not claiming that one or other of his various determinate conceptions approximates the real order of the world; certainly he is not claiming that one of these has a counterpart in reality. Indeed, at this point he is not even concerned with anything which might properly be called a conception of order. In brief, he is not arguing from a conception nor is he arguing that it has a counterpart. Instead, he is making the very different claim that a particular name or term necessarily has a reference. More specifically, he is claiming that "order", as here used, is a necessarily referring name or expression. Put another way, he is claiming that the world necessarily possesses order in the sense of "the way the world is, however that should prove to be". In the final analysis it is precisely this and nothing else which the scientist does and must mean by the term "order".

So used, this utterance has two important if perhaps controversial features. First, and as already suggested, it is a significant assertion or genuine factual claim about the world. This might be denied on the grounds that, since "order" is used to stand for the way the world is, the statement is therefore necessarily true. The assumption is that it could not therefore be a genuine assertion or fact. Such objections presuppose some distinction such as that of Hume between relations of ideas and matters of fact. But clearly this easy distinction is not beyond dispute. No one would argue that the statement "This is a triangle" does not assert a fact because "triangle" is the name we use for objects of the class referred to in this case by "this". Further, if "This is a triangle" states a fact when "This" stands for a triangle, so too does "This triangle is a triangle" when "This triangle" refers to the same figure. Whether an utterance states a fact is one question; whether it is necessarily true is another and a very different one. If we feel tempted to deny that a necessarily true statement can be a genuine assertion or claim, that is surely a sign that we need a notion of fact which is less invidious than the common and generally empiricist one.

But there could be another and perhaps more plausible reason for denying that this use expresses an assertion or claim. One might in fact be quite unable to imagine any point in making such a claim. It is very easy to sympathize with this objection; indeed, granted the scientist's use of "order", it is difficult not to do so. But it is clear that, so long as there are Humean critics of science, this use will always have a point. The teacher can and does say things like "This is a triangle", "A triangle has three interior angles", "X stands for a numerical value". He does this because he sometimes has to remind students of an elementary point they have forgotten. This third use of our model has precisely the same kind of function. It reminds the critic of the way in which the scientist uses the word "order"; it calls his attention to the fact that the world does and must have some one determinate shape. It reminds him of that elementary point upon the neglect of which his entire case is based.

The second feature of this use is closely connected with the first. The factual claim expressed therein is not, of course, a merely contingent one. Instead, and unlike most such claims, it is a necessary truth. What it asserts about the world is necessarily so. It is a claim which, in the sense intended, could not possibly be false. This is because the world could not conceivably lack order in the heuristic sense. To understand this use of the word, to grasp the logic of this utterance, is to know that it is necessarily true.

The claim that this utterance, so used, states a fact takes care of the first or *ontological* part of our description. But it is important to recognize the second and, particularly, to see their connection. The importance and role of the *linguistic* aspect can be put quite simply. Knowing that the world has and must have an order in the heuristic sense is not at all like knowing one or more of the ordinary empirical details of the world. It follows simply and directly from understanding the scientist's heuristic use of this term and its necessary connection with the world. In short, the utterance, and the truth of the utterance, follows from the heuristic use of the term. But, it must be added, this utterance is not in any sense a merely linguistic truth. The fact it asserts is no less a fact, and no less important for the fact, that it follows and follows necessarily from a certain use of a word. It is to underline and protect this truth that we have described this as the ontological-linguistic use.

We have deliberately chosen the term "'ontological-linguistic" but it is perhaps worth questioning the distinction which this description appears to assume. Recently we have been encouraged to draw a sharp line between the empirical and the linguistic but it seems possible that this line is largely illusory. Certainly one is tempted to ask whether claims such as "This is a triangle" are true in virtue of the nature of the object designated by "This" or because of the way in which we have decided to use the word "triangle".[9] Perhaps the distinction, at least in any final sense, is a fiction of a mind enchanted by the hope of breaking out of the prison of its own language. Perhaps we have been led astray by a now famous aphorism. Perhaps we now need to be freed from a peculiar, modern bewitchment. Perhaps we should say not "A cow is what the public calls a cow" but "A cow is a cow is a cow..." or, better, "A cow is what it is and we call it a cow".[10] In any event we need to see that the peculiarities in the use of "order" to which we have called attention do not in any

---

[9] Cf. "How do I know that this colour is red? – It would be an answer to say: 'I have learnt English'." Wittgenstein, *Philosophical Investigations*, Pt. I, 381.

[10] The original is, I think, from Wittgenstein. Unfortunately, I have lost the reference.

way impugn the status of this use of the utterance as a genuine, factual claim about the world.

It must now be clear how this third use of our model does in fact serve as the foundation of science. The condition of science is simply the fact that the world does and must have some one particular and determinate order, that it has something properly named or referred to by "order" in the heuristic sense. Science does not rest upon some merely contingent matter of fact. Its real and only necessary foundation is something that could not be other than it is; it is simply the presence of order in a sense which the world could not conceivably lack. This is the objective fact which makes this and any possible world a proper object for scientific investigation and which, in the final analysis, justifies this discipline. The role or function of the ontological-linguistic use of this utterance is simply to assert or call attention to the fact that the world necessarily possesses order in this sense. It is in thus using his utterance that the scientist states the foundation of his discipline. If this is not a direct answer to the philosophers' challenge it is at least a way of saying that the correct answer is very different from any that the Humean philosophers have thus far imagined.

Our ultimate aim in examining these various uses of our scientific model was to lay the basis for an answer to certain charges against religious claims and, more generally, belief. However, in the course of this examination we have uncovered some features of these uses which should help to clarify certain aspects of religious belief. These have already been indicated and can be summarized very briefly. Their application is obvious and is here indicated only in passing.

The first point concerns the question of the existence or reality of the various types of order with which, in different ways, the scientist is concerned. Put another way, it concerns the question of the status of these orders. By this is not meant the old and perhaps too simple question as to whether these orders are objective or, as some would hold, merely subjective. Essentially, the question is whether existence or reality, whatever its mode, can be ascribed to the determinate orders which the scientist describes or only to the heuristic order upon which his discipline is based.

Our considerations thus far make the answer to this question quite clear. The whole development of modern science suggests that we cannot conceive the various determinate orders described by science as actually existing in the world. We cannot, for example, think of Newtonian gravity as the, or, except in a very special and restricted sense, even a force or order in the universe. Put another way, we cannot regard this as a correct or adequate description of what is actually happening in the physical world. With a single possible exception, these descriptions are at best inadequate and premature accounts of the order which the world actually possesses. Such conceptions do not have a counterpart in reality and it is plainly misleading to speak of such orders as existing. On the other hand, it is clear that order in the heuristic sense can, does, and must exist. It is clear that this use of the term points to and links with something actually and necessarily present in the world. Hence, even in the sphere of science, we are left with the paradox that we must regard the various determinate orders as convenient fictions and ascribe reality only to an order which we cannot ourselves specify. *Mutatis mutandis*, the same is presumably true of our various uses of "God". It is, however, only fair to add that religion has long recognized that its essential object necessarily surpasses all human conceptions and therefore that these conclusions should hardly come as a surprise to any thoughtful believer.

This has interesting consequences for those claims asserting or implying the existence of these various orders. It is, for example, clear that the assertional use of an utterance involving a determinate order, whether empirical or metaphysical, could not be literally true. Or, rather, it is clear that only one such claim could be literally true. On the other hand, it is clear that the ontological-linguistic use of an utterance asserting the existence of order in the heuristic sense could be and, indeed, is strictly and literally true. Again, it is clear that claims of the former type are only contingently true while those of the latter are necessarily so. Finally, though the scientist might succeed in discovering the determinate order of the world, he could never know that he had actually done so. Because alternative explanations are always possible he could never be sure that his claim was in fact true. When, however, he asserts that the world possesses order in the heuristic sense he can and does know that his claim is true. In short, his heuristic use of the term and his ontological-linguistic use of his utterance, uses even the possibility of which the traditional dogmas deny, are, in the final analysis, the only ones not open to criticism. Again, *mutatis mutandis*, each of these claims would appear to be equally true of their various religious counterparts.

The next point concerns the relation of the scientist to his various claims. Here we can consider first the ontological-linguistic use which functions as the foundation of his discipline. Philosophers in the Humean tradition tend to see science as an essentially irrationalist affair and some at least speak of it as based upon an act of belief or faith. It is, however, now clear that this seriously misrepresents the actual situation of the scientist. Such terms are ordinarily and properly used in respect of something that might be other than it is, or, more correctly, which might be thought to be other than it is. We say that we assume or believe something at least partly because we can imagine what it would be like for the opposite to be the case. But the fact upon which science is based could not be other than it is. The order upon which science depends is one which the world could never lack. Nor can the scientist conceive of the world as possibly lacking order in this sense. It is therefore entirely misleading to speak of him as assuming the foundation of his discipline or as accepting it as a mere belief. He knows and has every right to claim that he knows the fact upon which, in the final analysis, his discipline rests. This, we shall argue, is equally true of the relation of the believer to the foundations of his belief.

Clearly the scientist has a quite different relation to his ordinary assertional claims involving the various determinate orders. In fact, he does not ordinarily assert or claim their existence or reality. He does not say that there actually is something in the universe corresponding to them; at most he regards them as convenient fictions and their existence as a working postulate. And yet he does in some sense assume their existence; in any event, his investigations presume that they are at least a partial reflection of the real order of the world. Their reality is for him a matter of belief or faith; at least, this is perhaps the best and most instructive way to describe his relationship to these orders. Perhaps, and in much the same way, it is just such determinate conceptions which are the proper object of belief or faith within religion.

The last three points are more immediately related to our present concerns. It is well known that most scientists are not much concerned to demonstrate the foundations of their discipline. They are in fact scarcely more concerned to do so than are most religious believers. But we have already seen that the ordinary scientist's complacency may not be entirely unjustified. The critics' charge is really a demand that he demonstrate that which, rightly understood, does not require or even admit of demonstration. Here, at least, demonstration is simply beside the point. This suggests that the same may also be true of the parallel charge against the religious believer.

The next point is closely connected with this. In recent years both scientists and philosophers have frequently spoken of science as a game. There is much merit in this suggestion and we would not think of simply dismissing it. It is however clear that, if it is a game, it is at least one of a very peculiar kind. For it is a game whose rules are grounded not simply in the way things are but, as we have seen, in the way in which they must be. In short, science is grounded in the strongest possible way. If the analogy holds, this must also be true of religion.

It is already clear that the scientist actually uses language in ways not allowed by the traditional philosophical dogmas underlying the charges with which we are here concerned. As we have seen, he is able significantly to assert and apply a predicate though unable to specify the attributes for which it stands. He can state a factual claim which, however, is necessarily true. He can make assertions about the world which are neither empirical nor metaphysical but which are in fact highly significant. He can speak of an order of the world the cash value of which he cannot however specify. It is surely unnecessary to point out that such actual instances constitute the strongest possible refutation of these dogmas. In any event, it is perhaps more relevant to observe that the fact that the scientist can use language in these ways constitutes a strong presumption for the view that the religious believer may be able to do likewise.

It now remains only to ask whether the scientist's utterances and, indeed, science itself can be cleared of the charges mentioned at the beginning of this chapter. It is clear, at least with respect to the first of these charges, that the question is in fact more complicated than first appears. As we have already attempted to make clear, it will not do simply to ask whether the scientist's utterance is itself falsifiable. His utterance has a variety of uses and we must ask which of these are falsifiable and which are not. Further, we must ask whether, given the use, unfalsifiability is a serious or even significant defect. We must ask whether it indicates real vacuity or pointlessness. Naturally, these answers must be given in terms of individual uses.

It is of course clear that this charge is scarcely appropriate to the scientist's second use of his utterance. A piece of self-instruction may be sound or ill-advised; it may be difficult or even impossible of implementation. But it cannot be true or false and its unfalsifiability is an entirely innocent feature following directly from its nature and function. Certainly it does not hinder this use from filling the role for which it is intended.

The situation is quite different in the case of the first use. Though this one can scarcely be true in the strict sense it nevertheless aims after truth. It attempts to make a factual claim. It is therefore falsifiable and, it might be added, repeatedly falsified. But, and this is a most important point, because of his approach to the subject, because he is constantly putting his material together in a new way, the scientist repeatedly furnishes a new determinate meaning for "order", a meaning which he urges in place of the one he has been forced to discard. Order(m) gives way to order(n) and this in turn to order(o) and so on. Evidence can tell and tell decisively against what he intends to assert but it does not and cannot tell finally against that utterance itself. Utterances like

"The world has order(m)" are repeatedly defeated but "The world has an order", just because it is a loose and elliptical form, is never subject to final defeat or falsification. And, it may be added, it is no worse for that. Certainly the incorrigibility of this utterance is no evidence that any instance of this particular use is in any way vacuous or meaningless.

The case of the third sense is, of course, quite different. Here the scientist is asserting a claim which is factual but one which is so with an important difference. He is not alleging that the world is some particular way; he is not making a claim which might be either supported or refuted by evidence. His is a claim which could not possibly be false. The world might lack any particular order; it might even lack the order it presently has: but it does not and cannot lack order as such. His claim is then essentially unfalsifiable. But, so far from being a defect, this is instead its real strength. It is this unfalsifiability which justifies the scientist's essential resolve to treat every event as pointing to the real nature of the world's order. It is this feature which makes it possible for this use to do the job for which it is intended.

The answer to the second or undemonstrated and indemonstrable charge involves only the scientist's third use of his utterance. This charge would indeed be serious if, as the Humean philosophers assume, science did in fact rest upon some merely contingent truth. Such matters of fact do indeed require demonstration and until it is forthcoming we may perhaps remain sceptical. But, as we have seen, science rests instead upon a very different sort of fact. To put the matter in the briefest possible way, the condition of science is simply that the world possess a feature it could not possibly lack. Science rests upon a fact which could not be other than it is or, at another level, upon a claim whose truth cannot properly be doubted. The world, in order to be a world, or indeed anything at all, must necessarily possess order in the heuristic sense. The conditions of science are, as we have seen, identical with those of existence. There is therefore no question of demonstrating these foundations, at least not in the sense which the critics seem to intend. The foundations which they offer are indeed undemonstrated and indemonstrable but this is not the case with the foundations upon which science actually rests. These foundations are claims which, in the relevant sense, are necessarily true. To understand their nature is to see that this charge is simply beside the point.

III

UNFALSIFIABLE AND VACUOUS

In the previous chapter we showed how science and its claims might be cleared of charges similar to those currently standing against religion. This preliminary exercise completed, we can now proceed to examine those charges with which we are here specifically concerned. The first is the unfalsifiability or, more adequately, the unfalsifiable and vacuous charge. This one, it will be recalled, holds that religious beliefs, though represented as factual truths, are in fact unfalsifiable. It claims that religious utterances are empty and vacuous in the sense that nothing is ever allowed to count against them; that, though they masquerade as factual claims, nothing is permitted to stand as a counter-instance. It is clear that this charge, if it can be sustained, casts doubt not only on these utterances but, equally, on the believer's claim to believe them. What, after all, can it mean to believe a claim which could never be falsified, which is compatible with any imaginable state of affairs? At least in any ordinary sense of "believe", it seems to mean nothing at all.

We have come already to the source of the critics' uneasiness, and no one can pretend that it is entirely unjustified. From their point of view, the believer seems guilty of bad faith. Though he plainly intends his claims as factual, he refuses to surrender them even in the face of conflicting evidence. We are not here concerned to deny that many believers do in fact behave in this way but we would point out that it is not at all surprising that they should do so. When, later, we have occasion to note the complexity of actual uses of religious claims this habit may come to seem less objectionable. For the moment it is perhaps sufficient to point out that the same philosophical beliefs which prompted the critics to identify "falsifiable" with "meaningful", together of course with the repeated advice of these same critics, have prompted believers to view their own claims as essentially and merely factual. It is then not surprising that those who have had little or no occasion to reflect upon the logical character of their utterances should have come to regard them as single claims of a straightforwardly factual character. But the fundamental question is not that of the views or conduct of some or even a majority of believers. It is, rather, whether and to what extent the believer's claims are unfalsifiable and, hence, as the critics charge, meaningless or vacuous.

Our underlying intention can be put in another way. No one is helped by asking the crude question whether a particular utterance is meaningful. Nor is anyone helped by asking, as philosophers are prone to ask, whether a given use of language is a proper one. In the hands of philosophers these too readily become confused with the question whether such claims and uses conform to our accepted notions. This indeed is the root of the so-called empiricist philosophers' difficulty with the assumptions of science just as, as we shall see, it is the source of their difficulty with religious claims. Because they knew how language must work they were incapable of discovering how it did in fact work. We hope to avoid this particular pitfall. We shall not ask whether religious claims are meaningful. Our aim is rather to understand and describe some of the more important kinds of meaning which such claims actually have.

The present chapter will consider the unfalsifiability charge with specific reference to "God is love" and, later, "I believe in God". Or, rather, it will do so with reference to the principal uses of these utterances. Each of these claims has certain idiocyncrasies but it is clear that they are characteristic of religious utterances in general. The first is the believer's most frequent private thought and claim; the second, the opening words of the Apostles' Creed. Of course, the Creed goes on to make many further claims but it is neither possible nor necessary to consider these here. This deliberately abbreviated form typifies religious claims and, like the first example, focuses attention upon that aspect which most troubles the critic.

As already implied, the sponsors of the unfalsifiability charge habitually fail to discriminate the various senses in which religious utterances are actually employed. The sorting out of these senses will therefore be one of the principal concerns of the present chapter. After these have been identified there will be time to ask which uses are falsifiable and which are not.

One further point. Whether these uses will actually pass the unfalsifiability test has not yet been determined, but the reader may rest assured that neither they nor our examples have been chosen with this end in view. Our chief aim is to report and describe some of the more important and distinctive uses of religious utterances. If any of these seem unnatural or strained this could be due to the fact that, perhaps under the influence of certain philosophers, we have learned to disregard some of the senses in which believers actually intend their utterances.

Though "God is love" shows some slight grammatical impropriety,[1] there are obvious reasons for beginning with this familiar utterance. Its form is very close to that of our model and simpler than that of the second example. Also, it is this claim which is most frequently and naturally cited in connection with this particular charge.

1

The believer's "God is love" has the same complex relation to religious belief and practice as our model has to the activities of the scientist. It is therefore used in three parallel situations and, hence, in three corresponding senses.

Of the various uses of "God is love" the first and most common

---

[1] Alasdair MacIntyre has somewhere pointed out that love is a relation and has proposed as an alternative "God is loving". We have however retained the believer's normal "God is love", both because it can perform all the functions open to the suggested emendation and because it seems possible that its slight grammatical impropriety may actually be revealing.

is the assertional one. Its purpose is to make a factual claim about God. The believer has in mind some determinate meaning for the word "love" and he intends to predicate this quality or character of God. This may be because he has recognized some event as an expression of this love or, alternatively, because some experience has brought him to a new and perhaps fuller understanding of its nature. Of course, he may feel that his conception of love is not entirely adequate; he may even insist that it does not and cannot do justice to the real nature of God's love. Nevertheless these sophisticated and proper doubts do not obtrude upon his normal use of this utterance. In the situation or context he uses "love" in a determinate sense and he consciously intends to assert this of God. His meaning can then be expressed as "God is love(m)".

Though this use of the utterance is perhaps not the most decisive or distinctive one, it is nevertheless of very great importance. Such uses play a prominent part in the life of worship and they constitute an important part of the beliefs of the religious man. It is, in fact, such claims which constitute what is usually called the content of belief. It is of such that we speak of someone as *believing that*.

We have described this as the assertional use of the utterance, and the believer clearly intends it in this way. Nevertheless this is not strictly correct. Because "love" may stand for a host of different determinate values the utterance, as here used, is not so much an assertion as a blank for a variety of possible assertions. This is central for the question of the unfalsifiability of this particular use.

A second and more decisive use of this utterance occurs in a very different kind of situation, a kind which is not uncommon in the life of the believer and which has even become classic in the literature. We have already provided our own special example: it is that of a young man who, having known only good fortune and happiness, now learns that he is dying of cancer. The question is that of the sense in which he would now use this utterance.

It is merely a prejudice to insist that in this situation such a person must intend "God is love" simply as a habitual and purely automatic response. And it prejudges the issue to assume that he must recognize his present situation as an expression of God's love, or that he intends his utterance as an assertion. In any event, linguistic form is a notoriously unreliable guide to actual use. In fact, there is no reason to suppose that the believer who uses this utterance in such situations actually intends a factual claim. Rather, I suggest, he is doing something quite different and, finally, much more important. He is in fact engaging in some far-reaching self-instruction. [2] He is enjoining himself to see this presently incomprehensible event as revealing, however darkly, something more of the nature of God's love. He is repeating the rules of his discipline and, at the same time, binding himself to accept these rules. He is using "love" in a heuristic sense. By the same token he is using the entire utterance in what we have called the self-instructional sense. His meaning is then best expressed as "I must treat all events as pointing to God's love(X)".

There are two points to be noted in passing. Firstly, there is no reason to suppose that the believer's present resolve is merely arbitrary and capricious. In all probability, he has had sufficient past experience of God's love, and been sufficiently surprised by its varied forms, to make this an entirely reasonable response. Secondly, no one supposes that all events must be a direct and transparent disclosure of God's love; certainly no one would argue that this was so in the case of our young victim. On the other hand, though such tragedies are not themselves a direct expression of that love, they are something without which human beings might never know the fuller measure of that love. In this sense then they are its dark and indirect revelation, and are rightly so regarded.

This use is typical of the religious believer and indicative of

[2] It might be argued that this activity is better described as self-pledging rather than as self-instruction; certainly it has some of the distinctive aspects of the former. However, it seems more correct to speak of self-pledging in connection with long-range policies and commitments and of self-instruction in particular cases in which the speaker is reminding himself to act in accordance with an earlier pledge. We have therefore described this as the self-instructional use and have translated it as, for example, "I must...".

a very important element in the religious life. Religion does not consist entirely in the holding of certain beliefs; equally important is the acceptance of a discipline to act in a certain way. And it is this which the believer undertakes when, in such situations, he deliberately says "God is love". He is steadying himself, binding himself to respond in a certain way. This may still be described as belief but it should be qualified as *belief in* rather than *belief that*.

As with our model, the third use of this utterance occurs in the face of criticism and, perhaps, self-doubt. The sceptical critic sees the young man's plight as clear proof that God is not love and as decisive evidence against the believer's claim. And perhaps the young man himself begins to doubt. Such situations bring out the distinctive character of the third and admittedly rare use of this utterance.

It might be thought that the believer is here claiming to see how everything, including his present misfortune, is indeed an instance of divine love. This would make his utterance a straightforwardly factual claim corresponding to the "metaphysical" use of the scientific model. But this use is open to the same objections as in the previous case. In any event the young man does not know the meaning or content of "love" in a way which would permit him to see how his condition squares with God's love. He is not in a position to see his misfortune as an expression of that love. Indeed, if he could so see it, he would not be in his present difficulty.

There is, of course, another obvious interpretation of this utterance. It might be argued that the young man is using "love" analogically. On this view he would take the highest conception of love which humans can know and apply this analogically to God. Now no doubt such terms are sometimes so used; no doubt many have been taught so to use them. I want only to suggest that they are not necessarily so used. Or rather, I want to suggest that in such situations they can be and often are used in another and very different sense.

That use has already been seen in the case of our scientific model. The scientist can say "The world has an order" even when he is unable to specify that order. And he can know that his utterance is true even when, in the ordinary sense, he does not know the meaning of "order". This is because, for the scientist, order is simply a copy of the way the world is. The believer's use of his utterance in this situation is exactly parallel. He does not know the meaning of "love" in the ordinary sense; he cannot produce an account of love of which his present situation is clearly an instance. He cannot therefore employ this term in its determinate sense. Nevertheless he does know that for him it is God's action alone which finally determines the true meaning of this term; this is the only thing which, as a believer, he will allow to determine this conception. He does not yet know its full meaning but he is quite clear about the rules for its determination. Because of this he can assert and know as true the claim "God is love" in a sense best expressed by the form "God is love(X)". In our own terms, he can and does use "love" in an heuristic sense and, equally, he can and does use the entire utterance in an ontological-linguistic sense. [3]

[3] Those who thus far have been merely uneasy about our assumption that the claims of the believer parallel those of the scientist will perhaps now feel that their initial misgivings have been fully justified. They will point out that whereas science presumably accords all events equal weight, religion marks out certain ones as revealed and accords these a normative status. They will, for example, cite the tradition that God's love has been fully and finally revealed in the life and death of Christ and will claim that when the Christian asserts "God is love" he does, in fact, know precisely what he means by "love". Now I have no wish to deny the peculiar role and importance of such disclosures; indeed, I would maintain that they are the primary data upon the basis of which the believer formulates his determinate conceptions. I do, however, wish to suggest that those who object to the comparison on the ground that religion appeals to "revelation" may not have thought sufficiently concerning the problems in this concept. Indeed, there is reason to believe that the situation of the scientist and that of the believer are essentially alike even in this respect. Science regards every single event as authoritative or "sacred" in the sense that it allows and even insists that a theory which cannot accommodate each and every event must be regarded as inadequate. It also recognizes that rare and unfamiliar events, if duly established, can have very great importance. They can be occasions for revising even the most widely accepted theories; they can be "revelations" of reality. At the same time we must recognize that, traditional formulations notwithstanding, what the believer has is not revelation *per se* but only his limited and inadequate perception of it. And this is all he could possibly have. This is clear on both epistemological and theologi-

A brief word in explanation of this description. The believer is indeed making a factual claim about God but one which, unlike ordinary factual claims, could not be false. The scientist's use of "order" is such that the world could not lack it. Similarly, at least at this point or extremity, the believer's use of "love" is such that God could not fail to show or express it. Of course, this does not bind God's action any more than "The world has an order" places a restriction upon nature. It is simply a way of saying that, for the believer, "love" is finally defined from the outside.

The preceding analysis suggests certain important and illuminating parallels between the orientation and responses of the believer and those of the scientist, and it may be helpful to indicate these explicitly. Both work with determinate conceptions which they intend to predicate of their objects but which they will, in appropriate circumstances, withdraw as inadequate. And, connected with this, both also employ their key concepts in a heuristic sense, *i.e.* as a marker to stand in for a meaning which is in some sense already fixed and which it is their primary concern to discover. To this end both are resolved to treat every event as relevant to the final determination of this concept. In neither case is this procedure arbitrary or strange; it is no mere convention or optional rule. Indeed, these disciplines can be carried on and

---

cal grounds. Christian theology has always acknowledged that we cannot fully grasp the nature of God and his love and the claim to revelation cannot in any way alter this. Clearly, then, it will not do to reject the comparison on the ground that the believer has access to revelation while the scientist does not.

There is one other small but important chink in the armour of the revelation claim. In many of its traditional forms at least, this claim reflects both inadequate respect and appreciation for the "revealing" event and a naive account of human knowledge. People repeatedly speak as if events such as the suffering of our young cancer victim were in direct and obvious conflict with the love which the Christian finds in the life and death of Christ but the fact is that, apart from some experience of such suffering, direct or vicarious, we should have only the most sentimental understanding of that love. A community in which such suffering was unknown would be quite incapable of understanding anything of its real depth and dimensions. We can in fact understand the revelation of God's love in Christ only to the extent that we have some experience of the suffering which it involved.

finally justified only to the extent that their key concepts are understood in a heuristic sense and their fundamental claims interpreted as necessary truths.

The results of this survey can be succinctly summarized. Like our model, "God is love" has three principal uses, uses we have called the assertional, the self-instructional and the ontological-linguistic, respectively. These can be expressed in ordinary language as follows: "God is love", "I must treat all events as pointing ultimately to the true nature of love", and "God's fundamental attitude is one of love". Or, in the symbolism we have suggested: "God is love(m)", "I must treat all events as part of the divine love(X)", and "God is love(X)". It now remains to comment briefly upon the falsifiability of these uses of this particular utterance.

Quite naturally these results precisely parallel those in the case of our model. At least so far as the believer's second use of his utterance is concerned, it is clear that the unfalsifiability charge is scarcely appropriate. The self-instruction to see all events as pointing ultimately to the true nature of God's love may be sound or ill-advised; it may be difficult or even incapable of implementation. But it cannot be either true or false, and the demand that this particular use should be falsifiable only shows that one has not grasped its peculiar nature.

The situation in respect of the first use is rather more complicated than might first appear. This is connected with the fact that "love" can be here used in a variety of different determinate senses. Of course the specific claim which the believer intends is always open to falsification. Assertions which specify the love of God for his creatures are falsifiable in principle and repeatedly falsified in fact. On the other hand, because this utterance, so used, is less an assertion in the strict sense than a blank for a variety of possible assertions, it is itself never subject to final and decisive falsification. The claim that God bears us a certain kind of love may be defeated or perhaps revealed as inadequate, but this does not mean that the believer must give up the term "love" or that he must withdraw the utterance-blank with which he first made this claim. Certain events can falsify "God is love(m)" but they do not rule out the formula "God is love" in which this claim is ordinarily expressed.

The third use is also unfalsifiable but for a quite different reason. It asserts that God's fundamental attitude to his creatures is one of love, but here "love" is conceived in such a way that this claim could not possibly be false. It is, in fact, the name for God's fundamental attitude, whatever that should prove to be. It is used in such a way that it makes no sense to ask if God is love or, for that matter, to assert that he is not. [4] The truth is that the believer accepts God's action as the touchstone for this concept; he agrees that his actions, past and present, shall determine what he means by "love". In short, this use of the utterance shows how the believer connects "God" and "love" and, rightly understood, is not even open to falsification.

2

Our second example "I believe in God" occurs in the same three contexts and has the same three principal uses. Though it differs from the preceding utterances in two minor aspects all three are, as we shall see, fundamentally alike.

The first of these differences has already been noted. Whereas the preceding utterances have a simple assertive form, "I believe in God..." is more rich and complex. It consists of two separate layers or aspects: a declarative aspect (or, perhaps better, form) expressed in "I believe..." and an assertive aspect or element which may be indicated as "...that God exists" [5] or, in certain

---

[4] This point can be illustrated with the following example. A very young child who had been reared in a religious if hardly pious home turned one day to her parents and, with an air of feigned and genial defiance, announced quite simply and firmly, "God doesn't love me". In fact, the impish gleam in her eye made it quite clear that she knew she was saying something roughly equivalent to "White is not white".

[5] The reader is warned that this is a tentative translation and may be later withdrawn. It seems clear that, as we shall argue, "exists" cannot be properly predicated of "God" in a determinate sense; whether it can when the latter is used in its heuristic sense is perhaps a more open question. These problems will be considered in chapter four.

situations, "... that there is a God" or words to this effect. Even this cursory analysis suggests the way in which the first aspect influences the second and, depending upon the context, makes the latter something quite distinct from the traditional "God exists". It also directs attention to the important fact that religious utterances are something more than the assertion of fact conceived as such. This is perhaps most obvious in the case of the second use where the declarative form actually functions as a reliable index to the intended sense. To a lesser extent this is also true in respect of the other two uses. In both these cases, particularly in the first, the form is important from a religious point of view. However, since we are here concerned only with what the believer intends to assert, we shall consider the form of his utterance only insofar as it serves to reveal the real nature of his claim.

There is one other obvious difference between "I believe in God..." and the preceding example. Whereas the latter deals with the nature of God the former appears, at least at first sight, to concern only his bare existence. But these questions are much more closely tied than is often supposed. In fact, and with one notable possible exception, the question whether God exists is unanswerable apart from at least certain assumptions concerning his nature. The two questions are in fact interdependent and this particular difference between these utterances is more apparent than real.

In fact, our two religious utterances are essentially similar. This is evident from the fact that those situations which cause problems for one of these utterances also cause the same kind of problems for the other. And it is further supported by the fact that our new example is normally used in the same three contexts as the preceding one.

The believer's normal and typical use of "I believe in God" is to declare his belief in some particular God. Stripped of its declarative form, it is to make the factual claim that God, as the believer now conceives him, does indeed exist. The God in question may be that of the believer's childhood or that of some sophisticated theologian; in either case he has some determinate conception in mind and intends to assert that something exists corresponding to this conception. His meaning is then best conveyed as "God(m) exists". And this of course is the assertional use of this utterance.

There is no doubt that, as a matter of fact, such claims and the belief expressed therein play an important and even indispensable part in the life and thought of the believer. But it would be entirely wrong to suppose that this is the whole story of his belief. Belief may well begin here but if it never moves beyond this point it can scarcely be worthy of that name.

Of course, this use of our utterance has the particular features and difficulties already noted. For example, while it is used to assert the existence of God, its determinate conception is necessarily inadequate and the claim cannot therefore be strictly true. On the other hand, though intended as an assertion or claim, this utterance as ordinarily expressed is not so much a factual claim as a blank for a set of such claims for all of which it is equally appropriate. As already explained, this radically effects the falsifiability of this use.

Like the previous example, "I believe in God" has a second and quite different use. Consider the situation of the young man who has just discovered that he is dying of cancer. Just as this man is not now in a position to see how God is love, neither is he able to see how his plight may be squared with God's existence. And, significantly, he does not say, "God exists". Instead, he says, "I believe in God". In so saying he is telling himself to undertake to see his plight as, together with the rest of experience, pointing to the true nature of the God who exists. He is using the term "God" in its heuristic sense and the utterance in its self-instructional one. This time he is saying, "I must treat all events as pointing to the real nature of God(X)".

This same instruction can of course be expressed in a different way. It can be put as "Understand 'God' in its heuristic sense" or, alternatively, "Allow the content of 'God' to be determined by events". This is simply the same resolution put in terms of the meaning of words.

This use of the utterance is at least as common as the first; in actual practice perhaps the two are set in a kind of balance within the life and thought of the believer. But whatever the relative frequency of this use, it is again clear that religious belief is something more than and different from commitment to certain merely factual claims. It is also *belief in*. To believe in this sense is to interpret events in a certain way. Or, rather, it is to commit oneself so to interpret them. It is to undertake a certain definite course of action. In short, belief, at least in this sense, does make a difference.

The two preceding uses normally occur within the context of worship, whether public or private. The third or *meta-religious* use [6] usually occurs outside such a context as, for example, when our young victim is surrounded by his critics and perhaps beset by his doubts. The critic wants to be shown how this tragedy can be reconciled with the existence of God. At the very least, he wants a conception of God with which this could be reconciled. And, one might suppose, nothing less can assure even the believer. But, notoriously, he cannot supply this conception and herein, of course, lies his problem.

The plight of the believer is, of course, precisely similar to that of the scientist who is required to justify his practice. And, not surprisingly, he responds in a precisely similar way. For the solution of his problem does not consist in claiming to see what plainly he does not see; it does not lie in pretending to have a meaning for "God" which will cover his tragedy. It consists

[6] There is, perhaps, some difficulty in the suggestion that this particular utterance can be used in this third sense. This will become more apparent when, shortly, we are forced to admit that the claim in question is not, strictly speaking, an item of belief. Taken literally, this would mean that the believer would be professing belief in something which is not properly a matter of belief. We have already tried to go some way to meet this difficulty by referring to this as a *meta*-religious use; later we shall attempt to make clear why this utterance, with its specifically declarative form, is not really appropriate in such circumstances. For the moment, however, we shall be content with the admission that it would be sufficient for our purposes if the believer simply used the familiar form "God exists". At least it would be if this form could be freed from its traditional interpretation as the statement of a merely contingent matter of fact; or, put another way, if it were read as "There is a Being properly referred to as God". This is, of course, also a possible translation of the assertive aspect of our own example.

rather in using the term "God" in its pristine and heuristic sense, in using it as a marker for "the Ultimate Reality, whatever that should prove to be". It consists in using or asserting this utterance not in its "metaphysical" but in what we have called its ontological-linguistic sense.

There is, of course, no question of the existence of God thus conceived. That there is such a God is a necessary and indubitable truth, a truth distorted in the traditional "God exists" but more adequately expressed in the form "God(X) exists". [7] In any event, this latter formulation makes it clear that one is not asserting the contingent existence of *a* being but rather the necessary existence of the ground of reality, and hence of Reality or Being as such.

Earlier we said that, in most cases, the question of the existence of God was generally inseparable from that of his nature. And certainly this is the case in the first use. But it is not so in the present one. The believer who intends "God(X) exists" is not laying claim to knowledge of the nature of God; indeed, he is tacitly insisting upon the inadequacy of such knowledge as he already has. Nevertheless, he is saying that God, thus conceived, does and must exist. And this insight is the real foundation of religion in precisely the same way as the realization that the world must have a similar sense of "order" is the real basis of science.

We have alleged that religious utterances are actually used in three separate and distinct senses. Before proceeding it may be well to offer some evidence for this claim, at least in respect of the less obvious cases. This is perhaps not necessary for the first use. Despite its difficulties everyone recognizes this as a common and familiar use of such utterances. Nor is it particularly necessary to argue at length for the second. This use reflects a central aspect of the religious life and one which, if generally neglected in philosophical accounts, is nevertheless acknowledged by all who truly understand the range of such life and belief. Concerning the third, however, there may be some doubt. This is not simply because traditional theories of language tell against the possibility of such

---

[7] We have already expressed our reservations concerning this particular formulation. See note 5 above.

use. Equally important is the realization that religious belief is in some important sense focused upon a determinate conception of God. This is a fact which is widely known and to which even specifically devotional writings abundantly testify. But religion has another different and equally important aspect. Though worship is indeed directed upon a determinate conception of God, it nevertheless acquires its distinctive quality and tone from the sure knowledge that God is something other than, and different from, any human conception of him. The worshipper necessarily "works" with his own conception of God but he is capable of real worship only to the extent that he realizes that God necessarily surpasses both his own and any possible human conception. Indeed, it is just this realization which marks the line between real worship and mere idolatry. [8] Even orthodox theology, itself perhaps tending in the opposite direction, makes this point with its insistence upon the infinity and essential incomprehensibility of God. This is therefore an essential and acknowledged aspect of the properly religious life. It is of course this aspect which underlies and is reflected in the third use of our examples.

It would no doubt be both interesting and instructive to consider the falsifiability of these different uses of this example, but this would perhaps prolong our discussion unduly. Equally important, the special problems raised by this example can be discussed in greater detail and with more point in the next chapter. We shall therefore proceed directly to the question of the falsifiability of religious utterances as such.

3

The charge before us is that religious utterances are unfalsifiable and, hence, meaningless or vacuous. The preceding analyses of the common uses of such utterances has shown that this charge is both crude and implausible. Indeed, it has made it clear that there are

[8] For another recent account of this important distinction see H. D. Lewis, "Worship and Idolatry", *Contemporary British Philosophy*, ed. H. D. Lewis (London, Allen & Unwin, 1956).

no utterances in the abstract but only specific uses of these utterances. The question then is whether these different uses are unfalsifiable and, if so, whether they are also vacuous.

The self-instructional use of religious utterances or beliefs is central to the religious life even in its narrowest aspect. But such beliefs, when so used, are not subject to falsification. A piece of self-instruction may be good or bad; it may be wise or ill-considered. It may even prove so difficult to follow that the believer forsakes both the task and the instruction enjoining it. Men do give up belief: for one reason or another they despair of reconciling events with the love and existence of God. Repeated failure in this endeavour would perhaps be a kind of analogue to but nevertheless not a case of falsification in the strict sense of that term. Even its demonstrated impossibility, assuming there could be such a demonstration, would not constitute such a falsification. The reason is simple. An injunction cannot be either true or false: it is not even the sort of thing which might be so. Hence the demand that this use be subject to falsification is simply mistaken. It betrays a confusion concerning the specific character of this use and, if urged against the utterance as such, suggests a failure to note the presence and importance of this use as an aspect or element of belief.

The assertional use of such utterances states or expresses a factual claim and is therefore properly subject to the falsifiability test. But the application of this test is less simple than one might imagine. Someone using an utterance in this sense is indeed culpable if he refuses to surrender his intended claim in the face of conflicting evidence. But, as already suggested, utterances when so used are not so much assertions as a blank or shorthand for a variety of assertions, a variety made possible by the fact that the key term in such utterances is really a variable for a number of different and distinct determinate conceptions. And because this use travels together with the self-instructional one, because the two are constantly set against each other, one determinate conception constantly replaces another and new factual claims are urged to replace those already defeated. Hence, while evidence can and does tell against any instance of this use, it cannot tell against the use itself. The believer's specific factual claims are frequently defeated, but the form in which these various claims are expressed is not itself ever subject to final defeat.

The ontological-linguistic use of religious utterances shows important differences from both the preceding ones. Because religious utterances, so used, assert a factual claim it might be supposed that they are proper candidates for the falsifiability test. But, as before, such utterances are factual with an important difference. Though factual in a perfectly proper sense, they are also, as we have insisted, both true and necessarily true. As here used, they could not be false; there is nothing which could conceivably tell against them. Hence the protest that such claims or beliefs are unfalsifiable is irrelevant and entirely beside the point. It is simply a fact and neither a defect nor a virtue. This feature is a consequence of its distinctive logic and its function as the real foundation of belief. It is therefore very strange to protest that this use is unfalsifiable. Indeed, those who press this charge simply show thereby that they fail to understand its nature.

The ostensible and avowed purpose of the falsifiability test was to provide a criterion of meaningfulness by which to separate significant claims from merely vacuous ones. The proposed procedure was simply to ask whether any conceivable empirical evidence could falsify the utterance in question. But this identifies meaningfulness with verifiability and so begs the question at issue. In fact, though none of the various uses of an utterance are readily and finally falsifiable, they are nevertheless very far indeed from being meaningless in any but the most technical and trivial sense. The next step is to show the kinds of meanings which these uses actually have.

It will be helpful to begin by underscoring a point which has emerged from our discussions. Religious belief is not simply assent to a set of propositions or claims. Rather, like science, it is an interpretative activity carried on in the light of certain beliefs and convictions. And, perhaps secretly, the critics understand this. Their fundamental complaint is not that the believer continues to assert certain claims; it is rather that, even in the face of evidence, he continues to act and respond in a particular way.

It is perhaps only fair to admit that there have been factors prompting philosophers to link meaninglessness with unfalsifiability. At least until very recently, philosophers held that one of their main tasks was to describe the world as it really was; in short, they saw themselves as concerned primarily with the articulation of factually true statements. More recently, at least in the Anglo-Saxon world, they have implicitly if unwittingly accepted scientific generalizations as the norm of proper or acceptable utterance. Of course there have been other factors but these are perhaps the chief reasons why recent philosophers have shown so little understanding of the rich multiplicity of language and the many diverse functions which it performs.

It should be obvious that none of the three uses of religious utterances here described are in fact meaningless or vacuous. This is certainly so in the case of the first or assertional use. As already explained, though the form of the believer's utterance cannot itself be falsified, his various assertional uses are not only open to falsification but, if he remains open and loyal to experience, are often falsified. But the meaning or point of this use has a very different source. It expresses the present ground of the believer's decisions, actions and, in a real sense, his way of life. This use is therefore immensely meaningful and important and it would be exceedingly strange to dismiss it as vacuous or pointless.

This is equally true with respect to the second or self-instructional use. This one expresses the rule according to which the believer interprets his life and experience; it is the instruction which prompts him to respond, and to continue to respond, in a certain way. That it is not even open to falsification is then relatively unimportant. The fact remains that it is far from being meaningless or vacuous save, of course, in a purely invidious sense with which we need not be concerned.

The third or ontological-linguistic use might seem to pose more of a problem. This is partly because of its great rarity and remoteness from daily experience. But even brief reflection reveals the point and importance of this use. It justifies the believer's primary rule according to which he interprets all events as pointing to the existence and nature of God. It is therefore the ultimate ground of those conceptions which the believer derives from this patterned response and upon which he bases his daily decisions and, finally, his style of life. In short, this particular use is no more meaningless or vacuous than either of the other two.

At the outset of this study the unfalsifiability charge was expressed in terms of the notion of belief and it is perhaps appropriate to conclude the consideration of this charge with some comment upon this notion. That it does make sense to speak of believing religious claims must surely now be evident. In the ordinary sense of "believe", one may believe a religious claim in its first sense; he may *believe* that what it alleges is in fact the case. And, in the sense explained, he may *believe in* a claim in its second sense. I should myself hold that the term "belief" is not sufficiently strong to be used in connection with the third sense. [9] It does not do justice to the particular manner in which the believer holds this sense. And it is not compatible with the fact that, in the sense intended, the claim in question could not possibly be false. But this is really only a question of how we are to describe the believer's relation to this sense. The important point is that this use is clearly significant and that it makes perfectly good sense to speak of someone as holding what is asserted therein.

This account would not be complete without a final but hardly damaging admission. In order to simplify the task of analysis we have spoken as though claims were always used in but one of their various senses. In actual practice, of course, these senses

---

[9] Of course there is no question of the possibility of commitment or adherence to this claim: the only question is how this attachment is to be described. There is of course the logical point that what is the foundation of all other beliefs cannot itself be a mere belief. But the normal and established usage of "belief" is the decisive consideration. Generally speaking, belief is an entertainment relation to a factual but nevertheless contingent claim; we say we believe something when we are able to imagine that the alleged state of affairs might be other than it is. We do not however say that we believe something which could not be other than it is. We do not speak of believing that one plus one equals two and this because the former is precisely what we mean by the latter. By the same token, neither can the believer be properly described as believing in the existence of the God who is the real ground and foundation of this faith: unlike the objects of his determinate assertions, this God could not not exist.

are frequently combined with one another. For example, the believer may intend his utterance in both its assertional and its self-instructional sense; he may even intend it in all of its senses. This means that actual uses are often much more rich and complex than our account suggests. It also means that their assessment is a very complicated matter. But it does not mean that our conclusions are in any way invalidated.

The charge before us has been answered, and it remains only to appraise the critics' attitude toward the conduct of the believer. Briefly, this attitude is one of annoyance and exasperation stemming from the fact that, as they suppose, the believer refuses to alter and, particularly, to surrender his belief even in the face of conflicting evidence. This the critics can neither understand nor accept and this is the real reason why they have fastened so firmly upon the notion of unfalsifiability. This goes to the very heart of their criticism of religious belief; indeed, this is what they regard as its central and fundamental flaw. We are perhaps now in a better position to decide whether this annoyance is justified. Indeed, we can perhaps now better understand the attitudes and positions of both the believer and his critics.

Of course, it would be a serious matter if the believer actually behaved as his critics imagine. In fact, however, many do not do so. Of course, believers do continue to speak of their faith as based upon revelation. They are not much inclined to tell the world of their own spiritual struggles nor, perhaps, to be entirely forthright about the drama of their own development. As members of a historic community, they continue to use traditional forms even for the expression of new insights and beliefs. These facts tend to convey the impression, particularly to outsiders, that religious belief is merely uncritical acceptance of certain static dogmas. Few judgements could be further from the truth. Believers find that their particular claims are falsified by events and they attempt to replace these by other claims having room for such events. They give up one sense of "love" in favour of another; they move from one conception of God to another more adequate to their experience. There is real development and change within a religious community and no one who has seriously studied the history of any living religion could possibly suppose otherwise.

But it is not simply that people change their particular beliefs; in certain cases at least they give up the posture of belief altogether. Faced with evidence which falsifies their present conceptions, and doubting their ability to articulate new ones, they decide to abandon the habit of treating events as pointing to the existence and nature of God together with the distinctive uses of their key concepts which justify this habit. In every significant sense, they cease to be believers. The kind of surrender for which the critics repeatedly ask does in fact take place. Of course, believers do not cease to be believers; but that is another and merely logical point.

The surrender of particular claims is relatively easy to understand, but what can be described as the surrender of belief as such is much more complicated. Here we can be helped by imagining a scientist who, perhaps after repeated failures, decides to renounce the scientific enterprise. That such a move is now very rare is unimportant; what matters is the nature of the reason behind it. Such a person would doubtlessly want to say that he had discovered that the world did not have an order after all. But this would be wrong and misleading. It would be much closer to the truth to say that, for perhaps perfectly good reasons, he simply despairs of discovering that order. The case of the believer who abandons his religious posture is precisely similar. His surrender is not the result of the discovery that, for example, there is no God. Searches do not reveal the absence of their object; in particular, they do not reveal the absence of God. One may of course discover that God(m) or(n) does not exist but it is in the nature of the case impossible to discover that there is no God(X). Strictly speaking, all that the erstwhile believer can discover is the inadequacy of his own determinate conceptions and particular claims. In fact, what really happens is that he despairs of making any kind of religious sense of his experience. For this there may be many reasons. His experiences may have been such as not to conform readily with accepted religious conceptions. He may lack the patience or intellectual ability to formulate new and more adequate conceptions. He may have identified religious belief with some particular claim which has now been called into question. He may emphasize his determinate conceptions at the expense of the heuristic use of key religious terms. In short, there can be reasons for the surrender of belief as such but these are essentially psychological. The final and logically conclusive defeat of religious belief is a fiction of the critics' imagination.

We have already echoed the critics' suspicion that the ordinary believer is too dull to appreciate the force of the charge against him. Now no one will praise stupidity, but it is important to understand at least some of the conditions of the believer's situation. For example, the language of religion is largely a borrowed one and it is not the primary task of the ordinary believer to discriminate the various senses in which he employs his utterances. Hence he may often intend these in a variety of senses without, perhaps, being able to say precisely which one he has most in mind. Further, he may well feel the peculiar quality of his underlying claim which we have attempted to indicate: though unable to express the matter clearly, he may at least dimly understand that the only claim to which he is finally committed is itself intrinsically irrefutable. These considerations are a mixed bag but, singly and together, they suggest that the believer may not be as intellectually obtuse as his critics imagine. They explain why he is not more excited by this particular charge; at least they show why he does not see every single apparent counter-instance as reason for announcing the abandonment of his faith.

But there are other equally good reasons for the believer's essentially conservative policy. Though the ordinary believer may be quite unable to state them, the critics' charge, despite its apparent plausibility, is in fact open to serious objections. Its invidious theory of meaning begs at the outset the question it presumes to settle. Its demand that belief should be falsifiable has been shown to be logically inconsistent. Its crude approach to the question of meaning has confused rather than clarified our understanding of both language and religious belief. But these standard objections are perhaps only a beginning. This charge considers only religious utterances as such and fails entirely to take account of the variety of their actual use. It treats religious claims as though they were merely empirical generalizations and so neglects both their distinctive logic and their characteristic use of terms. It assumes certain suspect philosophical dogmas about the way in which utterances and individual terms may function. It implicitly denies that language is actually used in a great variety of ways. To see this variety is to see that this charge will not do; to understand it is to have a better grasp of the ways in which language actually functions.

IV

UNDEMONSTRATED AND INDEMONSTRABLE

The first charge has been answered by showing that while the main uses of religious utterances are indeed unfalsifiable they are nevertheless very far from being meaningless or vacuous in any but a merely trivial sense. The second charge is specifically concerned with what it calls the foundations of religious belief. It holds that these are undemonstrated and indemonstrable. [1]

This charge has already been spelled out and can be restated very briefly. According to it, religious belief logically presupposes the acceptance of certain basic or fundamental assumptions. Some sponsors of this charge claim that these assumptions have not yet been demonstrated; others, taking a stronger line, claim to know that they are indemonstrable. All are, however, agreed that belief rests upon one or more such assumptions and that it can be maintained with philosophical respectability only if these are first established beyond reasonable doubt. They see religious belief as a giant structure whose logical foundations have yet to be secured. This view underlies their attitude to the believer. They hold that he is bound to justify these assumptions and, failing this, that he must in all honesty give up belief altogether.

There is perhaps little doubt that most believers would accept the main point of this charge. Many have lost confidence in the proofs for the existence of God, and even those who cling to them in private recognize that they no longer possess great apologetic

---

[1] This charge has been implicity assumed by many Anglo-Saxon philosophers writing recently on the philosophy of religion. In fact, it has been so common that the citing of any particular instance would be merely invidious.

value. We have been taught that religion is ultimately a matter of faith or belief rather than of sight or knowledge. Modern man has become extremely cautious about the possibility of demonstration or proof save, perhaps, in the realm of mathematics and logic. In our culture many believers are constantly tempted to represent their position as different and, particularly, as more strenuous than it actually is. These and other considerations prompt believers to accept and, perhaps, even to endorse this charge. But the real question is not what believers actually say; it is rather the very different question of what they ought to say. It is whether this charge is, in fact, justified. For reasons already suggested, this question can be answered best not by considering the traditional and theoretical accounts which believers are prone to repeat, but rather by examining and recording the way in which they actually use and intend their claims. Our high level accounts of belief have been seriously infected but we may still expect help from the way in which language is actually used.

As we shall argue, there is a basic confusion in this charge and, particularly, in the notion of a foundation of belief. This is at least suggested by the fact that the claims offered by the critics are themselves invariably items from within the body of religious belief. Like Hume's candidates, they are bound to fail the test for which they are offered. But this objection aside, it is clear that if this charge could be sustained religious belief would indeed be in serious difficulty. The believer can hardly be justified in accepting a body of propositions if he is quite unable to produce any kind of evidence for his belief in the assumptions upon which these are logically dependent. It is therefore clear that, at least so far as religious belief is concerned, this charge must be answered. It does not follow, however, that it must be answered in precisely the terms in which it is stated. In fact, it contains the same confusions as Hume's parallel charge against science [2] and is best answered in the same detailed and indirect way.

In spite of its confusions, Hume's position regarding the justification of the assumptions of science is clear and unambiguous.

---

[2] These have been discussed in chapter two, especially pp. 25-28 and 32-40.

He held all such claims were undemonstrated and, so far as he could see, indemonstrable. He believed, in fact, that his charge was unanswerable and he seems to have regarded this as the source of at least much of its strength. In fact it would be more reasonable to conclude that this points rather to its weakness. As already suggested, the fault is not always with the accused and the unanswerability of the charge tells less against science than against the particular way in which it was formulated. There are many reasons why Hume failed to see this but the immediate one is surely the fact that he misunderstood the nature of science and, hence, the real character of its foundation.

For whatever reasons, Hume supposed that science was possible only if this was in fact a certain sort of world; his was, as we have suggested, the "happy accident" account of science. Put another way, he supposed that science could be justified only by the establishment of certain factual claims which could themselves be established only by empirical means. It was this, of course, which drove him to the very plausible conclusion that therefore science could never be justified.

But Hume was caught in another and yet more fundamental confusion. Confusing science with its results, he supposed that the problem was to justify our belief in its conclusions. In fact, the real problem is rather to justify the basic order-finding activity of which its particular conclusions are simply a tentative and relatively unimportant by-product. This is a very different problem and one of whose peculiar nature Hume seems entirely unaware. The assumptions which he discusses might justify our confidence in scientific generalizations but they do nothing whatsoever to justify science as a particular kind of activity in the face of the world. Hume does not see that this is the problem and it is at least tolerably certain that he could not even have imagined its answer. As already suggested, this failure is due at least in part to certain of his philosophical convictions. He would not allow that we could have any knowledge of the world independently of experience. He would not admit that any statement of a matter of fact could be more than contingently true. Yet more fundamentally, if not so clearly, he did not imagine that words such as "order" might be properly used in other than a determinate sense.

The argument of the second chapter has shown that Hume's assumptions regarding science and its foundations are simply and fundamentally mistaken. Science does not depend upon the future actually resembling the past or upon every event actually having a cause; if, indeed, we could give any real sense to these imagined states of affairs or, for that matter, to their opposite. We now know that science is a possible and appropriate activity in respect of any body of data. It is a game which can always be played with any range of phenomena or any imaginable universe. It depends only upon the world's possession of some feature it could not possibly lack. Or, put another way, upon some fact that could not be other than it is. We can abstractly postulate a world for which scientific investigation would be impossible, but we can neither imagine nor describe it. And certainly it would be impossible for such a world to exist. Science is universal in its application and this not simply because, as we now recognize, highly successful prediction and explanation are possible upon the basis of admittedly and obviously premature pictures of reality. Basically, it is because the order with which science is fundamentally concerned is necessarily present in everything. It is because neither individual things nor the world in general can exist except in particular ways. It is because, in this respect at least, the condition of a thing's existing are one and the same with those for its being an object of science. Science does not require that the world have this shape or that. It requires only that it have some shape or other. And this is cannot conceivably lack.

The upshot of this is clear and indisputable. Hume's claim that science cannot be justified is confused and spurious. He mistook the nature of the problem and his charge gains much of its apparent plausibility from his use of certain key terms in an entirely nonscientific sense. He is asking the scientist to demonstrate something which, granted his view of the world, he could not intelligibly doubt. He is asking him to become agitated about a problem which, so long as he continues to be a scientist, he cannot even understand. Hume's whole case assumes that the foundations of science are merely contingent matters of fact which, because they are contingent, stand in need of empirical justification or demonstration. In fact, however, these foundations are necessary truths and hence the demand for demonstration, at least in any ordinary sense, is simply inappropriate and irrelevant. Of course it is necessary to know the truth of these claims but this is one and the same thing as understanding them in the sense in which they are intended. There is no question of demonstration for the simple reason that, in the sense intended, they could not possibly be false. It now remains to show that this is equally true of the real foundations of religious belief.

1

The charge that the foundations of religious belief are undemonstrated and indemonstrable is most frequently and perhaps naturally urged in respect of the existence of God. It is, however, equally relevant to a variety of claims concerning his nature. The consideration of such claims is important in itself and will underscore the close connection between the question of the existence of God and that of his nature. The believer's familiar and typical "God is love" will serve again as an example.

The significance of this charge in such cases is quite obvious. The critics hold that since "God is love" is a foundation of the believer's faith he may legitimately be called upon to demonstrate or establish it. They also hold that, if he is unable to do so, he ought in all honesty to abandon that faith. The question then is whether this claim really is undemonstrated and indemonstrable. Or, better, whether this charge is even appropriately directed against that use of this claim which actually serves as the foundation of his faith.

Such claims have a variety of uses [3] and it is important to concentrate upon the one which actually performs this particular function. This use has already been illustrated in the case of the

---

[3] The various uses of such claims have been discussed in chapter three, especially pp. 49–61. The present chapter presupposes these distinctions.

youthful cancer victim confronted with the critics' demand that he show cause why he should not surrender his belief. In fact, this example is a most useful one. It brings out clearly the sense in which the believer intends this claim when used as a foundation of his faith and, equally, the critics' very different interpretation of that claim. The latter is very important because this misreading not only prompts his charge but is also the real source of its apparent plausibility.

The critics' account of their victim's situation is a familiar one. They know that the believer has long held that God is love and they see him as continuing to assert this same claim in the face of contradictory evidence. They see him believing against the evidence and using faith as an excuse for maintaining what he secretly knows to be untrue. At best, they see him continuing to hope that his faith will some day be mysteriously justified. The critics reject all this and ask instead for a sense of "love" which will cover the situation, for some account which will save the appearances. Frequently the believer is unable to meet these demands and, not surprisingly, his critics interpret his continued belief as simple intellectual dishonesty.

In fact, the critics' account of this situation is itself due to their own interpretation of the believer's claim. They see belief as assent to certain simple factual claims about God, assume the foundation of belief to consist of one or more such claims, and interpret the believer's utterance accordingly. They see it as ascribing to God love of a particular and definite kind; as asserting, for example, that his attitude toward us is like that of an indulgent parent. In reality, it is this interpretation rather than the believer's claim as such which accounts for the critics' exasperation and, equally, for their conviction that the plight of the cancer victim actually calls these foundations into doubt or question.

There is no doubt that believers frequently use such claims in what we have already called their assertional sense. It is even true that believers in situations like that of the young cancer victim may so intend this claim and that they can and sometimes do supply a sense of "love" which meets the critics' objection. And it is further true that in such uses "love" can be a blank for a variety of determinate meanings and that this assertional use can therefore express all the varied claims which the believer intends throughout the course of his religious growth and development. This is the most common of all the believer's uses of "God is love" and these uses are extremely important. As assertions concerning the nature of God they express the real basis of his daily decisions and choices. Matters of belief, they express the immediate foundations of the believer's faith in what is perhaps its most significant sense. But, so used, they are not the foundations of his belief in the sense which the critics claim to seek. Nor are they the kind of claim the believer intends when he endeavours to meet this demand.

There is clear evidence that the believer does not intend the assertional use of this claim as a possible foundation of his faith. Recognizing that all his assertional claims are in principle falsifiable, the mature religious believer is always prepared to allow evidence to count against such claims. Like the scientist, however, he is almost completely unwilling to allow anything to count against the foundation of his faith. This is strong evidence that for the statement of these foundations the believer must intend a use other than the plainly assertional one.

In fact, there are strong logical considerations showing that the assertional use of such claims could not function as the foundation of belief and these obtain even if we neglect for the moment the ambiguity in the notion of such a foundation. The believer's conception of love is a developing one and the sense in which he intends this term in the assertional use of his claim must therefore change from time to time. His own assertions he recognizes as in principle inadequate and as, at best, a series of increasingly accurate approximations. The conceptions of love which he ascribes to God are ones which he has himself learned in the course of his own religious experience. And they can only be so learned. Finally, and most decisively, they are conceptions he has learned as a *result* of his adoption of religious belief. They are ones he has achieved *after* he has made the initial and momentous commitment with which we are here concerned. In short, the assertional use of this claim fails all the obvious tests for a possible foundation of belief.

The clue to the sense of this claim which really expresses the foundations of the believer's faith lies in his use of the key or operative term "love". This use, which we have already described as heuristic, may be put very briefly. This time the believer is no longer using it to stand for some single, determinate conception he has in mind, a conception which he might conceivably predicate of some subject, and which be could specify upon demand. Nor is he any longer using it for some specifiable quality or character which he intends to ascribe to God or for some determinate conception he has himself already fully formulated. This time his entire orientation is quite different. The *direction* of his thought, if one may so express it, is not from a concept to the world but rather from the world to a term or word. He is appealing not to his own conception of love but rather to the true meaning of that term as this is determined by external and objective circumstances. He knows that though "love" does indeed have a single, determinate and true meaning he cannot, for the moment at least, even in principle spell out that meaning. That being so, he now uses "love" as a pointer or token to stand in for this meaning. He is in fact using it as "X" is used in an algebraic equation, *i.e.* to stand in for some definite and determinate sense which, though not yet known, is nevertheless determined by the remainder of the formula in which it occurs. In the case of the believer the determining conditions are less readily identifiable but the situation is in principle the same. Here also there are objective determinants of the meaning and, just as the algebra student hopes to discover the value of X, the believer hopes that he will some day discover the meaning of "love". Until that time, however, he recognizes that he must sometimes be content to use this term in its heuristic sense.

It is worthy of note that though this use of "love" is comparatively rare it is nevertheless fundamental for religious belief. Even the ordinary and unsophisticated believer is apparently more confident of it than of his own determinate conceptions. This is clear from the fact that, when the two clash, it is almost always the former to which he continues to cling. This is a way of saying that the believer holds that it is God's action rather than his conception which finally defines this term. And this surely means that, for him, it is the heuristic rather than the determinate use of "love" which is primary and fundamental.

It is, of course, this distinctive use of "love" which is present in and informs that use of his claim with which the believer asserts the foundation of his faith. We have already described this as the ontological-linguistic use; recalling its function we might now also refer to this as its foundation use. In any event, in this use the believer is not asserting some spurious and unfounded generalization. He is not claiming that God is love in some sense he can presently specify. He is not pretending to be able to understand how his present situation is an instance of such love. What he is saying is in many ways similar to but, in the final analysis, very different from the ordinary, assertional use. And this difference is due to the fact that, though "love" here stands for a determinate quality or attitude, the speaker is unable, and knows that he is unable, to specify this sense. He is asserting that this situation actually is an instance of love but in a sense which he cannot yet describe or specify. More generally, he is asserting that God's actions, *i.e.* the events of this world, reveal the proper, final and true meaning of "love"; he is saying that it is these events which, rightly viewed, express the correct determinate sense of this word.

This particular use is and is intended as an assertion or claim and it is important to underline this fact. Nor is this status rendered doubtful by the fact that the believer cannot specify what, in the ordinary sense, he means by "love" or, indeed, by the fact that he uses "love" to stand for the attitude of God, whatever this should prove to be. Of course, it follows from this that what he intends could not conceivably be false; what he wishes to say could not be called into question by any possible evidence. But this does not prevent his utterance from being a significant and proper assertion. And, it is worth adding, it is just this feature which makes it possible for this use to function as a foundation of belief.

We have described this particular use as a factual claim or

assertion and, though it is admittedly one of a peculiar kind, it is nevertheless important to insist upon this description. But, as already suggested, it can equally well be thought of as asserting a connection between concepts; in this case, that between the concepts God and love as these are employed in, for example, normative Christian discourse. Indeed, it can be thought of as calling attention to this connection and as asserting the believer's assent thereto. But this does not in any way impugn its status as a foundation of belief. Indeed, it would be perfectly correct to describe this foundation as the perception that these two concepts were in fact connected in this particular way.

At the beginning of this chapter it was suggested that the critics' conception of a foundation of belief was perhaps not exactly transparent and clear. Since then it has become clear that their version of the believer's claim could not possibly serve as such a foundation. This version does not correspond to the believer's actual use and could never be established in the manner requisite for a foundation. And even if it could be established it would so serve only in the relatively trivial sense of providing the logical presupposition of other derived or secondary beliefs. In fact, it has become clear that the claims which the critics consider might be the result but could not possibly be the foundation of religious belief. It has also become clear that the sense which the believer actually intends in such situations does serve as a foundation in a very different and much more significant sense. Religion involves assent to certain beliefs but it is much more than such assent. It is also, as we have insisted, the resolve to act or respond in a certain way; in this case, it is the resolve to treat every event as revealing, however darkly, something more of the nature of God's love. It is, fundamentally, a quest for the correct determination of such concepts, a quest enjoined by the self-instructional use of the believer's claim and equally important, justified by the ontological-linguistic or foundation use of this same claim.[4] It is this which provides the believer's warrant for his overall religious response. And it does this whether we conceive this use as asserting a factual claim or

[4] The relationship or connection between these two uses is indicated on pp. 40, 52-54 and 58-61. Cf., also, chapter five, note 5.

as indicating the fundamental use of "love" in the Christian community. Nor is the latter any fatal admission: the use of words is, always and inevitably, a matter of fiat or decision.

It is clear that, like science, religion is and must be seen as an interpretative activity. It is also clear that the claim asserting its foundation is necessarily true and is able to function as a foundation just because it is intended and accepted as such. But the latter is equally true of algebra where the connections are yet more obvious. Taken out of context, we might find $X = 96 - (3 \times 2)$ "unintelligible" or even meaningless, or, given a value for X, we might decide that it was false. But the moment we recognize it as an equation such a judgement is impossible. Now the question of its truth no longer makes any sense. Because the value of the variable is determined by the combination of the remaining elements, this utterance is necessarily true. And this balance or necessary truth permits this formula to function as the statement of a problem just as its recognition enables the student to see it as a problem and proceed to its solution. But all this is equally true of the believer's "God is love". In its ordinary assertional use this claim is, of course, only contingently true; or rather, as has been suggested, it is, strictly speaking, necessarily false. But the use which states the ground or foundation of that activity called believing is quite different. Here "love" is intended heuristically, but because its actual determinate value is established by the implicitly specified defining conditions, the utterance, like the equation, is necessarily true. And this necessary truth functions here in the same way; it enables this claim to serve as a foundation of belief just as its recognition serves as the basis for the believer's attempt to determine more precisely the specifiable sense in which God is love. In algebra we can discover the value of the variable only by accepting the equation as necessarily true; in religion we discover something of the sense in which God is love by treating "God is love" in precisely the same way. The foundation of belief is not the arbitrary and groundless acceptance of some factual and contingent claim but rather the recognition of that odd but indubitable fact which justifies our resolve to treat experience in a certain way.

The answer to this charge is now clear at least with respect to the claim "God is love". Of course, if the believer intends its assertional use as the foundation of his belief, this charge is quite in order. Such claims require demonstration and in the absence of such we may reasonably be expected to surrender them. But, as is now clear, this is not the use which the believer does and must intend. When he wishes to state the foundations of his faith, he uses this claim in the very different ontological-linguistic sense, a sense in which, as has been shown, it could not possibly be false. It is therefore irrelevant to speak of demonstration or, for that matter, of falsification. The real foundation of religious belief is a claim which, rightly understood, does not require or even admit of demonstration. The charge that these foundations have not been and cannot be demonstrated is, then, simply beside the point and the moment this is seen it ceases to be interesting. At worst, it betrays a complete failure to understand the manifold and complex logic of such claims; at best, it is simply beside the point.

2

This same charge is most frequently and naturally urged with respect to what has traditionally been described as the existence of God. This is because the critics suppose all other religious beliefs to presuppose this existence and, equally, because they see this particular claim as a factual, contingent and obviously dubitable one. We shall attempt to answer this charge by describing the believer's true position in this matter. As before, we shall do so by attempting to discover the logic of his relevant use of the familiar "I believe in God...". The outline of our answer has already been indicated and can be expressed here quite briefly.

Before considering the different uses of this claim it will be helpful to note its peculiar form and some of the consequences which follow therefrom. These will stand out more clearly if we keep in mind the contrast with the philosophers' very different "God exists". As already suggested, the believer's utterance consists of two very different but equally important aspects or elements.

The first is its declarative aspect expressed in the words "believe". The importance of these prefatory words can be put quite simply. While actions are ultimately justified by the way the world is, our beliefs are logically justified by our acceptance of other logically prior beliefs. In the contemporary idiom, this formula makes the whole of what follows a performative utterance. This is the real force or point of "I believe...". Except perhaps in the case of the assertional use, it is certainly not to mark what follows as being in any way uncertain or doubtful.

It is tempting to interpret the second or content aspect of this utterance in a way which might be expressed as "...that God exists" or, perhaps, "...that there is a God". But this would be quite wrong. The utterance does not contain the term "exists" or any of its variants nor does it have the form of an ordinary existence claim. Nor is this any accident. As already implied, and as will be shortly argued, even the assertional use of this claim cannot be interpreted as a simple or straightforward existence claim. But this is equally and, for the moment, more relevantly true of the ontological-linguistic or foundation use. This is due in part to the peculiarities of the predicate "exists" and hence to the relatively complicated nature of such claims. But the real difficulty is that "exists" cannot be appropriately joined with "God" used in the heuristic sense.[5]

It is, of course, obvious that this claim is used most frequently in what we have called its assertional sense. The believer has in mind a particular and determinate conception of God and intends to assert the reality of a Being corresponding thereto. Despite its obvious difficulties, this claim can be so used even by persons such as our unfortunate cancer victim. And such uses express fundamental beliefs which are of great importance. They state the real and immediate basis of the believer's decisions, and hence the foundation of his belief in a sense perhaps even more important than that with which the critics profess to be concerned. Never-

---

[5] This crucial point appears to have been overlooked in most of the discussions of what has traditionally been called the existence of God.

theless, this use does not and cannot express that foundation: at most it can provide an illuminating contrast to the one which actually fulfills this function.

This use cannot serve as a foundation for precisely the same reasons as Hume's candidates cannot justify science. The belief expressed therein is essentially corrigible and could never be known with the certainty requisite for such a foundation. Such belief undergoes continual development whereas the foundation of belief must, by its very nature, be constant and unchanging. Finally, the various beliefs expressed in this use are accepted only after and as a result of the adoption of belief, and therefore clearly cannot be its foundation or justification.

Another point, to which we shall shortly return, implies this same conclusion. Though the believer lives by his determinate conceptions of God he knows that these cannot be taken as adequate; though he assumes that this God exists he also secretly knows that such claims cannot be taken as literally true. It follows therefore that his assertional uses, however important, cannot state the foundation with which we are here concerned. By the same token, it follows that believers can surrender their various determinate conceptions of God, together with their corresponding existence claims, without surrendering religious belief as such.

This point can be put with specific reference to Christian belief. The foundation of such belief is not the believer's conception or, for that matter, even the historic Christian conception of God. By the same token, neither is it the existence of a Being corresponding to these conceptions. This is not due to any peculiarity of Christianity or religion as such; indeed, precisely the same kind of thing is equally true of science. The real foundation of Christianity, as of any other religious belief, at least in the sense with which we are here concerned, is not properly conceived as a conception at all nor, indeed, as an existence claim involving such a conception. It is rather the insight that God necessarily surpasses all our conceptions; that, as already suggested, the word "God" can be properly used only in its heuristic sense. It is the insight that the God with which religion is essentially concerned could not not exist. It is this which provides the believer's confidence in what is only inadequately expressed as "the existence of God". It is this which provides the foundation for his continuing search and quest for a more adequate conception of God. In the final analysis it is this alone which marks the boundary between idolatry and religion.

This means that, as in each of the earlier cases, it is the ontological-linguistic use of this claim which states the foundation of different heuristic sense; a sense which, so far as it can be express- to stand for some determinate conception but rather in its quite different heuristic sense; a sense which, so far as it can be expressed, might be put as the Ultimate Reality or, perhaps, the Source of Reality, whatever that should prove to be. Hence in this use the believer is declaring his confidence that something actually corresponds to "God" in this sense. The question of the foundation of his belief is then that of the grounds of this confidence. But about these grounds there can be no doubt. The existence of the counterpart of a determinate conception of God is at best a contingent matter but the reality of God understood in the heuristic sense is a necessary truth.

This comparison admits of further development. Though it can never be conclusive, there could always be evidence in support of belief in the existence of the various determinate orders described by science. Similarly, though it can never be conclusive, there could always be evidence supporting belief in the existence of the various determinate Gods found in different religions. But with respect to the heuristic uses upon which science and religion are based, there can be no question of evidence or empirical pointing. In neither case are there any simple empirical facts which might be urged as supporting evidence. Nor is this a really serious problem. "Order" and "God", in the sense in which these serve as the respective foundations of their disciplines, are necessarily referring expressions and we have only to know their use to know that there must be something corresponding thereto. It is impossible that the world should lack order in the sense with which science is fundamentally concerned. In precisely the same way, it is impossible that there should be nothing corresponding to the use of "God" upon which religion is based. The believer who expresses his belief in

God in this sense is, among other things, asserting a claim which could not possibly be false.

There are important differences between the assertional and the present use and, again, between the traditional proofs for the existence of God and the kind of "proof" to which we have been pointing. Each of the former cases alleges the existence of a being corresponding to some determinate conception; the latter turns upon the use of a word in a sense such that it could not lack a counterpart. This is why it is misleading to speak of this as an existence claim and why it is much nearer the truth to say that "God" is here used as a necessarily referring expression.

The contrast can be expressed in terms of the following simple example. The philosophers have considered religious belief after the model of a wild animal hunt. [6] They have supposed that it was unreasonable to set forth until there was a guarantee or, at the very least, a very strong assurance that there was indeed an animal in one's allotted territory. In fact, however, religious belief is much more like the game of identifying the largest elephant in a herd already before us. Provided only that there is such a herd, the expression "the largest elephant in the herd" must necessarily have a reference. Again, provided only that there is something which is real (and it is merely philosophical in the bad sense to dispute this point) the expression "God", used in the heuristic sense, must also have an actual counterpart. This is not to say that there necessarily exists a being corresponding to any of our determinate conceptions; it is to say only that there necessarily is something rightly and properly referred to as God. The order with which the scientist is concerned is something the world could not lack and, in precisely the same way, the God with whom the believer is fundamentally concerned could not not exist. Big game safaris may indeed require the labours of advance scouts but it is impossible that the religious enterprise should ever be inappropriate or pointless.

[6] This is true even of Wisdom's sophisticated and influential "Gods" which implicitly treats the question of the existence of God as like the question whether there really is an unseen gardener who, perhaps secretly, tends the plot by night. This, of course, is very much like the question whether there really is a wild animal in my allotted territory.

This example may also help to clarify the sense in which God may be conceived as necessary. Of course it is not necessary that the particular elephant which happens to be largest should exist. Nor is it necessary that this particular elephant should be the largest. All that is necessary, and even here there are difficulties, is that some one elephant in the herd should answer this description. In the same way, and to return to our earlier notation, it is not necessary that the God(m) who happens to be God(X) should exist; that existence is never necessary guarantees this fact. Nor is it necessary that the God(m) who happens to be God(X) should be such. All that is necessary is that something correspond to God(X). [7] As here used, this expression cannot fail of reference. It is in this sense and in this sense alone that it is proper to speak of God as a necessary being and of "God" as a necessarily referring expression.

This account of the foundations of belief can be summarized very briefly. In all relevant aspects, the position of the believer is precisely akin to that of the scientist. The latter does not know that the world in fact has this or that determinate order but he does know that it has and must have order in the sense with which he is fundamentally concerned. And he knows this without, as it were, looking at the world for supporting evidence. In the same way the believer does not know that there is a Being corresponding to any of the philosophers' determinate conceptions. But he does know that back of the world there is and must be an Ultimate Reality. Of course, he may reject this and all such determinations as mere anthropomorphisms. But this is finally beside the point. He still knows that there is and must be something which corresponds to his heuristic use of "God". He still knows that this term, so used, is a necessarily referring expression. Hence for the religious believer, so long as he is a believer, the "existence" of God cannot even be intelligibly doubted.

---

[7] This notation is set forth and explained on pp. 18f. It is used in connection with our scientific model on pp. 28-31 and in connection with religious claims on pp. 49-61.

3

The two claims already considered are those of which the critics complain most frequently; they are also typical of those upon which religious belief is actually based. Hence the way is open for a more general formulation of the answer to this second charge. First, however, we must look at some of the assumptions regarding religious belief which it presupposes. Not surprisingly, these are very similar to the assumptions underlying the Humean charge against science.

It is commonly assumed that religious belief is a matter of assent to a series of dogmatic propositions. This is why the critics assume that the real problem is the establishment of the factual and allegedly contingent claim or claims upon which these propositions logically rest. In fact, however, religion is much more adequately conceived as an interpretation of life and reality. It is an ongoing attempt to discover a solution to a problem; in brief, it is, like science, a pursuit, quest or activity. This helps to explain the ambiguity in the critics' notion of a foundation of religious belief. Of course, assent to propositions requires assent to those upon which they are logically based; this is indisputable but points only to a relatively trivial sense of the word "foundation". However, belief conceived as an activity requires a foundation in a very different and much more full-blooded sense. It requires something which will justify this activity, something which will make it rational, reasonable and coherent. And it is precisely this which the ontological-linguistic or foundation use of the believer's claim provides. The scientist attempts to interpret every event as an expression of the order of the world and his justification for doing so is just that the shape which the world actually has is, in the final analysis, just what he does and must mean by "order". In precisely the same way the believer interprets every event as compatible with the love and existence of God and is justified in so doing because it is just the shape of these events which point to and determine what, again in the final analysis, he means by "love" and "God". The ontological-linguistic use of his claims justifies this practice by declaring that these terms are here used in their heuristic sense. Or, if this seems more acceptable, by calling attention to a fact which, in the sense intended, could not possibly be false.

Another assumption informing this charge is that religious belief is possible only if this is in fact a certain kind of world or, more specifically, only if God proves to be a certain kind of being and loves us in a particular way. Hence the critics' emphasis upon the prior establishment of some contingent, factual claim and their insistence upon the possibility of its falsification. This demand seems perfectly plausible but there are unanswerable objections. The logical difficulties have already been noted; if granted, this would imply the contradiction that one must first accept a particular assertional claim before one could be justified in doing so. The fact of religious development points in the same direction. Contemporary man accepts claims concerning the nature of God which his ancestors would have rejected as preposterous and there is every reason to suppose that our own successors will entertain beliefs which we cannot now even imagine. Finally, religion itself recognizes this as an insistence that God should obligingly conform to our own preconceptions and it brands all resulting belief as a form of idolatry. And rightly so for, at least in this particular respect, the formal conditions of religion are precisely similar to those of science. The Humean philosophers notwithstanding, science does not require that this should be some particular sort of world. Its only condition is one which could not possibly fail to obtain, *viz.*, that the world should be some kind or other. Neither does religion require that God should correspond to our preconceptions of him or that he should love us in the particular way we think most appropriate. It too requires only a condition which cannot fail to obtain, *viz.*, that there should be something corresponding to the heuristic use of the term "God" and that in and through the events of the world we should be able to detect his underlying attitude toward the creation.

The third of these assumptions is that religious belief, together with its foundation, must be at least subject to falsification and that, failing this, it is in some sense defective or spurious. But we have already seen that this is not true of the foundations of science.

No scientist would allow for a moment that any event, however strange, could possibly falsify his fundamental and underlying claim that the world has an order. And it is just because he intends and accepts his claim as unfalsifiable that it is able to provide the foundation for his attempt further and more precisely to determine that order. Its unfalsifiability, so far from being a defect, is in fact a condition of its doing the job for which it is intended. But all this is equally true of the believer's corresponding claims. Of course he allows that his assertional uses can be and constantly are falsified. But he does not and cannot allow that this might be true of the foundation use of his claims. He intends and accepts these as unfalsifiable and is entirely correct in doing so. And this is not simply because it is only as unfalsifiable that his claim can provide a justification for his activity. Most fundamentally it is because, in the only sense of his terms to which he is finally committed, his claim could not possibly be false.

It should now be possible to understand and evaluate this charge more clearly. Because of their own conception of religious belief, and ultimately perhaps because of their empiricist dogmas about language, the critics see the believer as committed to certain factual and contingent claims which, in the nature of the case, could never be adequately established. Naturally, therefore, they hold that the foundations of belief are undemonstrated and indemonstrable. But the question is not that of the foundation of belief as these critics imagine it; it is rather the very different question of the foundation of belief as it really is. It is that of the foundation of belief as an ongoing, interpretative activity. As in the case of science, that foundation is of the strongest possible kind. It is not simply a fact; it is, rather, a fact which could not be other than it is. At another level, it is a claim which, in the sense required and intended, could not possibly be false.

All this follows from the peculiar character of the believer's utterances in their ontological-linguistic or foundation use. So used, these utterances have one distinctive and overriding feature. Because their key or operative terms are employed in a heuristic sense, these claims could not possibly be false. To understand them in the sense in which they are required and intended is one and the same thing as to see that they are necessarily true. Hence it is entirely wrong to speak of someone as simply believing or assuming the truth of such claims. Their truth is built into them and, quite simply, to grasp their peculiar logic is to know that they are true. Those who persist in seeking assurances concerning their truth simply confess that they have not understood their nature. With respect to all such claims there is and can be no question of truth or, indeed, of proof. Nor, by the same token, can there be one of demonstration. The undemonstrated and indemonstrable charge is a demand for something already implicit in such claims, something we perceive the moment we understand their logic and function. Hence this demand is irrelevant or, perhaps, mistaken. If it has seemed plausible that is only because it mistakes the foundation of religion in precisely the same way as its counterpart mistakes that of science.

This answer can be phrased in a way which tells more directly against the critics. Of course, on their own behalf they can claim that their account of the foundations of religious belief is shared by most believers. They can say that the use upon which they have fastened is the most typical and, perhaps in some sense, the most important one in the life of the believer. They can protest that the theories of language to which they have implicity subscribed are not their own invention but have been endemic thoughout the whole of the empiricist tradition. But the fact remains that their demand is an impossible one. They are guilty of the same metaphysical cravings which Hume and his followers exhibited in the face of science and, like their predecessors, they must learn to live with these appetites unsatisfied. Religion is not based upon some merely empirical facts which, though derived from experience, might somehow miraculously be established prior to such experience. The foundation of religion is a particular and peculiar use of its own key terms and while the critics may reject this use this does not mean that such a foundation has not been established. Religion also has its moves and it will not do for the critics to complain that these do not conform to their demands and expectations. In this matter, critic and believer are separated by the use of a word. Granted the critic's use of "God" there is no way of meeting his demand but, equally, granted the believer's use, there is no way of stating it. Perhaps the most important task for the philosopher is simply to call attention to this fact. This answer surely helps to explain the attitude of many believers. The philosophical critics profess to be puzzled and are certainly annoyed that their prospective victims show so little interest in meeting their challenge. Now we would not claim that all believers would in fact subscribe to the account of the foundations of belief here suggested. And certainly we do not intend to claim that many could or would spell it out in terms as articulate or, perhaps, contrived as the ones we have offered. We are however convinced that this is a substantially correct description of the believer's unvarnished experience and that those who have not been corrupted will recognize it as such. For the truth is that for the claims to which the believer is finally committed, demonstration is simply irrelevant. And it is just possible that it may be this insight, rather than any native indolence or stupidity, which really underlies the believer's lack of interest in the charge we have been discussing.

V

CONCLUDING REMARKS

The charges with which this study was specifically concerned have been answered and it now remains only to say something of the account of religious belief assumed by these answers and to comment upon the case for belief thus conceived. As our model from science plays an important role in both cases it will be well to begin by attempting to allay the apprehensions of those who still resist the suggestion that religion is somehow fundamentally like science. Of course this is not the whole of the story but in fact the comparison points directly to some of its most important and interesting aspects.

It may be said at the outset that this analogy has not been accepted from any undue reverence for science or, most certainly, in an attempt to capitalize upon its current prestige. The fact that science may soon lose its present favoured position rules out any such attempt as tactically unwise. The real reason is the conviction that religion and science have certain essential and fundamental resemblances. The fact that the Judaic-Christian religion is the deepest cultural source of modern science is only the sign of their connection. Basically, both are interpretative activities proceeding according to the same necessary and fundamental rules of the human understanding. Their differences notwithstanding, they are historically continuous and their underlying similarities are even more important than their obvious differences.

This particular analogy may also be justified in another way. Christian theology once provided the culture's interpretation of reality but in our time this role has been taken over by science. Whether the latter does or can do the job as adequately is another question; the fact remains that it is science which informs the vision of contemporary man. Further, it is science, not religion, which in our time has managed to make clear the logic of its claims. These facts go far to explain the peculiar value of a model from this realm.

1

In the present context it is both impossible and unnecessary to describe in full the nature and complexity of religious belief. Indeed, it will suffice to note only those aspects of belief assumed by our earlier answers. We shall therefore consider the lessons to be derived from our model and examine in a more general way those features particularly linked with the various uses of religious claims. In both cases we shall follow the same order as in the original.

As in the case of our model, the first point concerns the ascription of existence or reality to God in the various senses of that term with which the believer is concerned. This is not the question whether it is ever appropriate or helpful to speak of God as existing but rather whether "exists", if it be allowed at all, is to be conjoined with the determinate or with the heuristic sense of "God". The parallels with our scientific model are striking and obvious. On the one hand it is clear that we cannot ascribe existence to any of our determinate conceptions of God; this is equally clear from the fact that we cannot regard any of these as adequately or completely describing his nature. On the other hand, it is clear that we must think of God in the heuristic sense as "existing" and this despite the fact that, in the ordinary sense of "mean", we cannot here say what we mean either by "God" or by "exists". The paradox here mirrors the one already discovered in science: our determinate conceptions of God must be regarded as convenient fictions while the heuristic use which we cannot specify is the only one which can be thought of as having an actual counterpart. Of course, as earlier suggested, it is only fair to add that this particular truth has long been recognized by religion. Indeed, it has always known that its object was, in the final analysis, properly incomprehensible. This said, there is no reason why science should not now be used to drive home some of the consequences of this insight.

As before, these facts have important consequences for the nature of the speaker's various claims. The assertional claim expressed by an utterance involving determinate terms cannot be literally true; or, rather, only one such claim could be literally true. On the other hand, the claim expressed by the ontological-linguistic use of such an utterance could be, and indeed is, strictly and literally true. Again, claims of the former type could only be contigently true while those of the latter are necessarily so. Finally, even if the believer did succeed in formulating an assertional claim which was literally true he could not, in the nature of the case, know that it was so. However, when he asserts claims employing terms in their heuristic sense, he can and does know that these are true. In short, his heuristic use of terms and his ontological-linguistic use of utterances are the only ones not finally open to criticism. These are his only uses which cannot be shown even in principle to be wrong and mistaken. These set the boundary of all that can be properly said about God.[1]

Of course, these facts are reflected in the relation of the believer to his ordinary assertional claims. Here his attitude is very much like that of the scientist. The latter assumes that his determinate conceptions of order approximate to the order of the world but he does not suppose that any of these are its exact and literal copy. His experiments presuppose the essential correctness of his conceptions but he assumes that these are but premature pictures of the way the world really is. The believer's stake in his conceptions is obviously greater but his response is very similar. Though he bases his choices upon his determinate conceptions, he does not really hold that their objects actually exist. Put another way, he does not assert that these conceptions

---

[1] I exclude, of course, statements about God in which terms are used, as it is said, analogically. I do so partly because I have never found an adequate *justification* of such use and partly because I think that, for the believer, it is the God-use rather than the common sense one which is primary and, perhaps, "literal".

have real or actual counterparts. He does not, for example, say that there actually exists a God corresponding to his conceptions. And this fact of usage is no accident. Though his conceptions are working postulates he recognizes that they are also convenient and necessary fictions. Hence his attitude toward his own assertional claims remains tentative and ambiguous. As his commonest use of his most characteristic utterance suggests, their truth is for him simply a matter of belief.[2]

Naturally the believer has a very different relation to the ontological-linguistic use of his claims. Here, again, his attitude is similar to that of the scientist. The latter knows that the world necessarily possesses order in the heuristic sense and he therefore knows as absolutely certain the use of his claim asserting that this is so. In the same way, the believer knows that the key term in the ontological-linguistic use of his claims is a necessarily referring expression and that his claim, so used, is therefore necessarily true. And this is no mere matter of faith or belief. It is instead a claim about which he is absolutely certain. His use of the performative formula in "I believe in God..." is then, at least in such cases, to be taken not as indicating a doubt or uncertainty but rather as confessing the fact that he has resolved to see the world and to use language in a certain way.

As in the case of the scientist these two very different relations point to two important features of religious belief. The latter reminds us that the foundations of religious belief are necessarily true and that they are intended and accepted by the believer as such. For him, these foundations are self-evident truths which he cannot even conceive as doubtful. It is therefore clear that the foundations of belief are certain and that belief itself is not irrational. At least, it is no more so than is the parallel discipline of science.

The former consideration points to an equally important aspect of belief. In this respect also the believer is very close to the scien-

---

[2] I mean, of course, his ordinary or assertional use of "I believe in God...". This utterance does not include the term "exists" or any of its variants and cannot be tortured into an existence claim. In most contexts, this use represents the believer's statement of his working faith.

tist. With his assertional claims he too attempts to state the truth about the reality with which he is concerned and he too is deeply committed to his account. Its truth or, at least, its substantial adequacy is a matter of the greatest importance to him. But in spite of this he knows that the claims and insights upon which he must act are not literally true. He knows that these are merely the best account that he can give at the moment and that in the final analysis he must be content to regard these as mere working hypotheses. He is however prepared to act, confident that his partial insights will, if conscientiously followed, lead him to other and more adequate ones. Like the scientist, he moves forward upon the basis of conceptions which he recognizes as less than entirely true. He knows that, in a real sense, he lives in the dark. But, in the language of poetry, he also knows that, for his purposes, the dark is light enough.

If now we recall the believer's self-instructional use of his claim we may perhaps imagine something of the real complexity of religious belief. The fact is that the believer uses one and the same utterance to remind himself to respond in a certain way, to assert a claim to whose truth he is committed but whose fundamental inadequacy he is forced to recognize and, at least in certain cases, to state a fact which he could not even begin to doubt. Further, two and perhaps even all these senses may be intended in any particular instance. It will be well to bear this in mind as we proceed to discuss the aspects of belief associated with these various uses.

Both the preceding analogies and our own earlier account of the various uses of religious claims show that religious belief does not begin with or rest finally upon some determinate and allegedly complete conception of God. It does not consist simply in assent to certain propositions dogmatically held in the face of conflicting evidence. It is not mere pious hoping in the face of admitted counter-instances. It is not a dogmatic stance which remains possible only so long as God conveniently conforms to our expectations. It does not preclude the possibility of doubt or the recognition of experiences which falsify certain of the believer's claims. More generally, religious belief is a complex condition or commitment with many interwoven strands and elements. Some of its more important features are here set forth as they appear in connection with the believer's different uses.

As is clear from the believer's first or assertional use, religious belief does of course involve certain factual claims. Typically these employ their key terms in a determinate sense and are assertions concerning the existence and nature of God. They are however quite unlike ordinary claims concerning the existence and nature of, say, some material object; the believer's relationship to them is therefore very different. Whereas he claims that God(m) exists or that God is love(m) he knows, both on the basis or past experience and religious insight, that these conceptions are only partially correct and that his claims cannot therefore be strictly true.[3] This is part of what is meant by saying that such claims are matters of belief or faith.

But there is another aspect which is at least equally important. For the believer such claims are not merely or even primarily items of mere abstract assent. They are rather matters of existential commitment in the proper sense of that term. They are the bases upon which the believer acts and by which he orders his life. This is the other and equally important aspect of faith or belief as it appears in this connection.

These two aspects of faith suggest an answer to the widely held view that it is simply an imaginary faculty by which believers claim to hold what they in fact know to be untrue. Of course, there is no doubt that the practice and, perhaps particularly, the reports of believers afford much evidence for this charge. But it is now clear that the believer need not be simply asserting on the one hand what he denies on the other. Indeed, it is clear that he at least is forced to live by conceptions and claims which he nevertheless knows to be inadequate. The recognition that this is so is

---

[3] The insight that the believer's determinate concepts cannot be wholly adequate or his assertional claims strictly true gives support and perhaps new meaning to an emphasis which runs through existentialism from Kierkegaard to Tillich. This is usually expressed by saying that belief is an understanding which objectifies that which defies objectification. This is, in fact, a very apt description of one aspect of the believer's determinate concepts.

at least part of what may be rightly called the tension in the life of faith.

These same features help to explain the believer's complex attitude toward his own assertional claims. Because he knows that his determinate conceptions cannot adequately mirror their object he is bound to recognize that his claims are always subject to revision. On the other hand, because his life has been based upon these claims he is naturally reluctant to surrender them without good reason. This is why he is always prepared to revise his claims in the light of counter evidence and, equally, why he is always hesitant in doing so.

It is clear that the believer's determinate conceptions play an important role in his choices and hence in what may be called his practical worship. These same conceptions also have an equally important place in his formal worship. Of course, the believer does not worship these conceptions; or, more to the point, he does not worship their object. A being whose nature can be fully and completely specified cannot be an object or focus of worship in its proper sense. Such an attitude is possible only in respect of a nature recognized as genuinely beyond our comprehension. We are capable of worship only so far as our determinate conceptions are conjoined with and overruled by heuristic ones. It is the latter which makes true reverence possible but it is the former which offers the mind something upon which to fasten. The believer does not worship the object of his determinate conceptions but he does worship God in and through them. They are intellectual images or icons through which his worship is channeled.

There is one important qualification to this account. It suggests, plausibly but wrongly, that religious belief is concerned simply and exclusively with God. The nature and extent of this error can be put simply and succinctly by a reinterpretation of the classical "proofs" for the existence of God. What they really demonstrate is that there is an essential equivalence between believing in the existence of a certain God and believing certain things about the world. More generally, they suggest that there is an essential tie between belief about God and belief about the world. Put another way, they show that if religious belief is merely "religious" it is not really belief at all. To this it is necessary only to add that significant belief about God also involves certain beliefs about the nature of meaning and hence about ways in which language can actually function. But this leads on to our later uses.

Fortunately those aspects of religious belief linked with the remaining uses of religious language can be expressed more briefly. The second or self-instructional use, for example, shows clearly that religious belief is something much more than mere assent to a number of determinate conceptions or assertional claims. Such items are practically and immediately important but they are on every count much less fundamental than the believer's resolve to treat all reality and experience as pointing to the nature of the Ultimate Reality or Being of the world. It is, of course, this resolve which accounts for the real continuity within historical religions such as Judaism and Christianity.

This basic feature can be expressed in another way. Religious belief is fundamentally an interpretative activity; it is an attempt to achieve an increasingly adequate grasp of the nature of its object. Of course, it differs from science in certain important respects. It does not restrict itself to "public" and repeatable events. It does not content itself with understanding purely in terms of what have been historically known as efficient causes. It does not confine itself to the physical universe but, through an understanding of that universe, seeks to discover the nature of the reality which lies behind it. These important differences help to mark the boundary between science and religion but at the same time they also show their essential continuity. They show that both are interpretative activities governed by the rule that everything is to be seen as an expression of some wider, single whole.

It is of course clear that this aspect of belief is not in the least meaningless or vacuous. It is the believer's fundamental rule and it governs his response to all events. It explains why he treats every event as pointing to and expressive of the nature and reality of God.

Of course, this element is not a matter of belief in the ordinary sense. The use in question is not a factual claim and cannot be either true or false. Its role is rather to recommend a certain course of action. It is something to which one commits oneself. We have already marked this by saying that it is a matter of *belief in*.

The believer's acceptance of such self-instruction points to a different but important sense of the word "faith". This can be brought out by considering the case of a believer who has had an experience which he cannot reconcile with his present conception of God. He might insist upon his conception and, in one way or another, attempt to deny the reality or relevance of the experience. In that event, we might speak of him as having faith in his conception. But this is an uninteresting and indefensible sense of the term. Imagine, however, that he makes a quite different response. Recalling his rule, he recognizes this experience as telling against his conception and he resolves that it shall have a share in the shaping of his future beliefs. In doing so, he has shown himself open to events and confident that God will not mislead him. He has shown that his underlying commitment is to the truth, whatever that should prove to be. In traditional language, he has shown a willingness to let God be God. Faith in this sense is one of the essential elements of religious belief. It is the underlying trust which enables the believer to question and revise all his assertional claims.

The importance of this underlying commitment or faith is quite obvious. It is the real source of growth and development within a religious tradition. It is the reason why religious belief has evolved in the past and why we must expect that it will continue to do so in the future. Its importance for the individual is equally clear. It is what keeps the believer from mistaking his conceptions for the reality to which they are intended to point. It is what prevents all belief from lapsing finally into idolatry.

This consideration of the more common uses of religious claims has pointed to certain aspects of belief in its specific or narrower sense. These are elements in respect of which the believer might rightly be said to have belief or faith. We turn now to the foundations of religious belief and hence to its consideration in a wider sense. This will involve matters which, as already indicated, are not items of belief or faith in the strict or proper sense.

Our account of the third or *meta-* use of the believer's claims has already made clear the nature of the foundation of the believer's faith. Such belief is not based upon one or more of the traditional or metaphysical proofs for the existence of God. Nor is it based upon any merely contingent factual claim. It does not rest upon some determinate conception of God. It is not even based upon a conception in the ordinary sense of that term. Of course historical religions work with determinate conceptions of God but their nature and development plainly shows that their real foundation is what we have called a heuristic conception of God, or rather, the reality corresponding thereto. The reality of God thus conceived is not a matter of belief; for the believer it is rather an absolute certainty following from the fact that "God" is here used as a necessarily referring expression. It is this use or, alternatively, the fact corresponding to this use, which accounts for the believer's apparently unshakeable confidence in his faith. Equally important, it is this alone which, in the final analysis, explains and renders intelligible belief both as worship[4] and as interpretative activity.[5]

This account of religious belief has had its point of departure in some lessons made clear by science and in the three main uses of religious language which we have distinguished. But it is perhaps worth adding that it does justice to certain familiar facts and claims. It accounts for the obvious complexity of religious belief.

[4] Of course worship requires both determinate conceptions of God and the heuristic sense of him as essentially beyond any such conceptions. But it is the latter alone which makes possible what is distinctive in the attitude of reverence and worship.

Kierkegaard, or rather his pseudonym Climacus, has pointed indirectly to the necessity of the heuristic use of concepts in worship and, specifically, in prayer. "So I am bound to thank God... if I thank God for the good which I know is a good, I make a fool of God... And yet I am bound to thank God for that which I know is a good, which, however, I am not able to know." *Concluding Unscientific Postscript,* p. 158.

[5] This follows from what is ordinarily meant by understanding. As already shown, science requires the use of "order", or conceivably that of some other term, in its properly heuristic sense. In this it reflects the operation of the understanding and, ultimately, what we mean by this particular term. Quite simply, understanding is seeing things and events in terms of a wider whole; it is seeing them as expressions of some one underlying reality. Hence it presupposes the use of some term in this necessarily all-embracing sense. This, very briefly, is why religious belief as an interpretative activity requires the use of "God" in its heuristic sense.

It explains how the distinctive attitude of worship is possible. It gives content, even on the intellectual side, to belief as a discipline. It shows or at least suggests the foundation of belief as an interpretative activity. It explains why believers give up both their particular beliefs and belief as a whole and, equally, why they are so hesitant and cautious in doing so. Finally, it accepts both the essential incomprehensibility of God and our ability to speak about him and it does so in terms of two uses of terms which, taken together, help to show how language actually touches the world. Of course, we do not claim that this is a complete account of religious belief but we think it does justice to those aspects with which we are here particularly concerned.

It would be a relatively simple matter to give this account an honorable and even impressive ancestry and this perhaps not so much in spite as because of its similarities with science. The polytheism of its environment notwithstanding, the Bible sees and stresses the importance of seeing God as essentially One. It insists that his nature is beyond our understanding and that all human conceptions of him are subject to further revision. Job's "though he slay me yet will I trust him" is the classic expression of a particular religious response but it is clear that both Jesus and his disciples were forced to re-think their conceptions in the light of their experience. Christianity has consistently represented itself as a discipline and as a way of life. The Church has generally held that the acceptance of belief involves both reason and risk. Such support could easily be further strengthened but it is more to the point to consider the case for belief thus conceived.

2

There can be little doubt that most belief, like most unbelief, is due to a combination of historical, cultural, sociological, psychological and even professional considerations. None of these are, however, our present concern. We are not asking why people do in fact believe; we are not even asking why they conceive and represent themselves as believers. Ours is the very different question why should anyone believe. Why should anyone adopt the stance and accept the burden of belief? What justification could there possibly be for such a move?

Of course, in one sense the real answer to this question has already been given. That answer lies in the nature of the foundation of such belief. It lies in the fact that this foundation is not simply a fact, but, the strongest possible case, a fact which could not be other than it is. It lies in the fact that the focus or concern of belief is God in a sense such that he could not not be. By definition, such a God demands worship and requires belief. Hence the foundation of belief is also its real justification.

Of course, there is an obvious reply to this move. The argument quite clearly hangs upon this peculiar heuristic use of "God"; it might even be said that this use begs the question it presumes to settle. This is, in a sense, true and we have already insisted upon it. But in fact the point is stronger than this reply assumes. For the question at issue is not the reality of this God or that but rather the reality of God in the peculiar sense with which religion is and must be concerned. And about the reality of this God there cannot really be any doubt.

This can be put in another way. It might be said that the believer's heuristic use of "God" begs the question and that his defence is simply a rephrasing of his position. And this might be answered by saying that, in the same way, the critics' failure to come to terms with this use is simply a refusal to face this question. But this would miss a crucial aspect of the situation. The question is not that of the justification of belief as the critics imagine it but, rather, that of the justification of belief as it actually and necessarily is. It is therefore up to the critics to show that this use of "God" is illegitimate. In this connection it is worth recalling that, so far from being a mere accident, this particular use is a condition of belief both as worship and as interpretative activity.

In the preceding chapter we spoke of the believer and his critic as separated by the use of a word. This was a way of saying that, the above objection notwithstanding, the critic can always ask why *he* should accept this use. This is the basic question and we must now try to state its answer.

This answer may become clearer if we begin by asking why anyone should adopt the scientist's fundamental use of "order" and, more generally, his characteristic attitude toward the world. Of course, there are cultural, pragmatic and even personal reasons for doing so but these, we have agreed, are now beside the point. The question is not that of the causes which might prompt one to adopt this attitude but rather the reasons or defences he might legitimately offer for doing so. Put thus, the answer seems quite plain. There is no absolute justification for the adoption of this attitude but one who is committed to the enterprise of understanding can conditionally justify this choice on the ground that science is the most disciplined expression of the human attempt to understand what is usually referred to as the world in which we live. Though he cannot finally justify his commitment to understanding, he can appeal to this commitment to justify his adoption of the scientific attitude. The situation appears to be very similar in the case of religious belief. There is no absolute and unconditional justification for belief as such. The believer may adopt a religious approach to the world but there is no argument by which he can rationally compel others to do likewise. He can, however, defend his position as following from his commitment to the enterprise of understanding and he can argue that those who reject it confess thereby that, to this extent, they have forsaken this enterprise. The justification for belief is like that of science; in both cases it is finally conditional. But there is one important difference. While both science and religion aim at an understanding of reality, the former, by its own nature and admission, is content with a limited and restricted account while the latter continues to strive for a total and unrestricted interpretation. Its drive for understanding is in every way more comprehensive and ambitious. It follows, therefore, that the commitment which really justifies the adoption of the scientific attitude points yet more strongly to the acceptance of religious belief.

It seems quite certain that this justification of belief will not satisfy either the critics or the "hard-line" believers both of whom have a vested interest in misrepresenting belief and, particularly, the nature of its justification. The critics will not settle for anything less than what they take to be absolute and unconditional proof; they are not likely to be satisfied even by the logical demonstration that such proof is in the nature of the case impossible. And the "hard-line" believers will not settle for anything less than an unconditional justification for their stand. Still under the spell of the rationalist dream, they want to be able to demonstrate the truth and necessity of their position. We are, however, content to appeal to the very different tradition that the believer walks by faith and not by sight. This view has survived even the Church's once sanguine optimism about the proofs and we shall be satisfied if our account does justice to this insight. More generally, we shall be satisfied if it has helped to distinguish between those aspects of religious belief which are necessarily a matter of faith and those which, once grasped, cannot even reasonably be doubted.

It would be quite wrong to see this account of belief and its justification as an attempt to come to terms with contemporary religious and theological fashion or, for that matter, with any of the other prejudices of the time. It is, of course, true that this age is very different from previous ones and that religious belief is now undergoing what many Christians at least regard as an unfortunate if perhaps necessary retrenchment. But this is a misleading interpretation of the present situation. The religious tradition of the past was mistakenly imperialistic and it is important that all remaining traces of this attitude be obliterated. The present retrenchment is not a misfortune but an opportunity. When religious belief loses the corpulence acquired in the days of its false prosperity, its real nature may then be more apparent.

It remains only to offer two final comments. Early in this study we suggested that the charges with which it was concerned were relatively recent and, perhaps overcome by the spirit of contemporary philosophy, that they were more fundamental and searching than those urged against religion in the past. The suggestion was that, helped by new and sophisticated techniques, our modern critics had begun to ask questions the answers to which their predecessors had simply taken for granted. There is no doubt a certain amount of truth in this but the answers we have uncovered suggest a very different possibility. They suggest that such charges have come to the fore in our time not primarily because of an increased sophistication but because of the failure to understand the various ways in which language actually functions and, behind this, the perhaps unwitting acceptance of certain traditional and generally empiricist theories in this regard. Certainly there is reason to believe that the latter are the chief source of both the current popularity and the apparent plausibility of such charges.

The final point is closely connected with this. Though this study was described as an attempt to answer two charges against religious belief, it has not been intended simply as a defense of such belief. Indeed, it has been at least equally concerned to dispute or, at least, to call into question certain familiar philosophical theories. Of course it has not attempted a detailed or point-by-point refutation. This was only partly because such refutation would inevitably and finally require the more or less adequate presentation of alternative theories. The real reason for our procedure was the conviction that these theories have arisen from the wilful neglect of the interesting and troublesome cases and that the best answer was therefore to provide some clear counter-instances. We hope that in doing so we may have helped to open some windows upon the world of language. Nor is this finally irrelevant to the defense of religious belief; as suggested earlier, real belief in God is closely linked with the holding of certain beliefs about the world and, perhaps particularly, with a more adequate understanding of the ways in which language actually functions.

STUDIES IN PHILOSOPHY

1. Nathan Rotenstreich: *Humanism in the Contemporary Era.* 1963. 171 pp. ƒ 23.—

2. Troy Wilson Organ: *The Self in the Indian Philosophy.* 1964. 184 pp. ƒ 26.—

3. P. Allan Carlsson: *Butler's Ethics.* 1964. 196 pp. ƒ 25.—

5. Lowell Nissen: *John Dewey's Theory of Inquiry and Truth.* 1966. 112 pp. ƒ 16.—

6. Ronald D. Milo: *Aristotle on Practical Knowledge and Weakness of Will.* 1966. 114 pp. ƒ 17.—

7. F. Warren Rempel: *The Role of Value in Karl Mannheim's Sociology of Knowledge.* 1965. 125 pp. ƒ 17,—

8. Ralph Philip Joly: *The Human Person in a Philosophy of Education.* 1965. 147 pp. ƒ 17.—

9. G. D. Bowne: *The Philosophy of Logic, 1880-1908.* 1966. 157 pp. ƒ 19.50

10. Joe K. Fugate: *The Psychological Basis of Herder's Aesthetics.* 1966. 303 pp. ƒ 32.50

11. John J. Fitzgerald: *Peirce's Theory of Signs as Foundation for Pragmatism.* 1966. 182 pp. ƒ 23.—

12. Allen Lacy: *Miguel de Unamuno: The Rhetoric of Existence.* 1967. 289 pp. ƒ 32,—

14. David L. Perry: *The Concept of Pleasure.* 1967. 224 pp. ƒ 25.—

16. Fred D. Newman: *Explanation by Description: An Essay on Historical Methodology.* 1968. 104 pp. ƒ 14.—

18. Arnolds Grava: *A Structural Inquiry into the Symbolic Representation of Ideas.* 1969. 176 pp. ƒ 24.—

23. Dhirendra Sharma: *The Differentiation Theory of Meaning in Indian Logic.* 1969. 120 pp. ƒ 21.—

MOUTON · PUBLISHERS THE · HAGUE